God Bless You Cam as you grow each day in your Spiritual life. You have our Prayers Everett

God Bless you Helen

I enjoyed being in Jr High S.S. class with you Mike M.

When You Walk Through Green Pastures ...
Stick to the Path

Blessings To You My Little Friend May God Keep You in The Hollow of his hand Dan

God Bless you, We're looking forward to Myf & having you be a part! Doug & Kris

Have Fun in H.S.

Maurice Be Good

God be with you Leela Snyder

May God bless & guide you Leroy yoder

God Bless You! Clara & Paul

When You Walk Through Green Pastures ... Stick to the Path

Devotions on the Book of Psalms

Martha Bolton

SERVANT PUBLICATIONS
ANN ARBOR, MICHIGAN

© 2000 by Martha Bolton
All rights reserved.

Unless otherwise indicated all Scripture quotations are from the Holy
Bible, New International Version, © 1973, 1978, 1984 by International
Bible Society. Used by permission of Zondervan Publishing House. All
rights reserved.

Vine Books is an imprint of Servant Publications especially designed to
serve evangelical Christians.

Published by Servant Publications
P.O. Box 8617
Ann Arbor, Michigan 48107

Cover design: Paz Design Group
Cover illustration: Pat Binder

00 01 02 03 10 9 8 7 6 5 4 3 2 1

Printed in the United States of America
ISBN 1-56955-170-7

Cataloging-in-Publication Data on file at the Library of Congress.

Contents

1. Charades

I was at a party recently where two girls spent most of the evening laughing and conversing with one another like long lost friends. They recalled this incident and that, and undoubtedly were having more fun than anyone else at the party.

When it came time for one of them to leave, they hugged, promised to keep in touch, and then the one girl went on her way. No sooner had the door closed behind her, when the other girl said, "I can't stand her!"

Say what? The entire evening was a charade? The laughter, the hug, the friendship—all phony?

Unfortunately, not all of the world's great actors are working in film, in television, or on the stage. Some of them are just ordinary people like you and me.

When Jesus said we would be known by our love, he wasn't referring to our dramatic abilities. He meant it would be real, so evident to those around us that not one trace of it would be suspect. In other words, that hug we give someone, the "Love" we sign at the bottom of our cards, or the famous "I'll be praying for you, friend" mean absolutely nothing. When it comes to loving our brother, what matters to God is the love we show people after the door closes behind them.

Thoughts to Ponder

Have you ever faked a friendship? Why do you think you did it?

Would you say you're a loyal friend, or one who waits until the door closes behind someone to show your true feelings?

Bumper Sticker for the Day

> **The only love that's a fact
> is the love you show behind someone's back.**

Scripture to Stand On

Do not drag me away with the wicked, with those who do evil, who speak cordially with their neighbors but harbor malice in their hearts.

PSALM 28:3

Hello Again, Lord ...

Lord, your commandment to "love one another" doesn't end with "but only to their faces." Help us to remember that.

2. Instant Messenger

One of the neat things about e-mail is Instant Messenger. While you're on-line, a "Buddy" can interrupt whatever you happen to be doing and ask to communicate directly with you. You then have the option of either accepting or ignoring the invitation to chat.

Usually the interruptions are welcomed. When working late into the night, it's kind of fun to get an occasional hello from someone who's also up working. There are times, though, when the interruption comes at an inopportune time, so we choose to ignore it. Without even knowing what the message is, we continue with our own work, and eventually the "Buddy" signs off.

If we listen, we can sometimes "hear" God's Instant Messenger. He'll interrupt whatever it is we're working on at the moment and ask if we'd like to talk. It's up to us to either accept his invitation or ignore it. Too often we choose the latter. We leave him hanging there, waiting for us to have a simple chat or a meaningful conversation with him, yet we're too busy answering other e-mail to be bothered. We press "Ignore" and continue with our work, until eventually our Buddy quits interrupting.

Maybe it's time to press "Accept" instead.

Thoughts to Ponder

Do you accept God's "Instant Messages" the minute he wants to talk to you?

When God wants to talk to you, why do you think it's a good idea to drop everything and listen?

Bumper Sticker for the Day

> **Talk to God. He's been on hold long enough.**

Scripture to Stand On

I wait for the Lord, my soul waits, and in his word I put my hope.

PSALM 130:5

Hello Again, Lord ...

Lord, forgive me for the times when I haven't answered your call.

3. If You Knew ...

If you knew your child wouldn't live to see his fortieth birthday, would you still choose to become a parent?

If someone warned you that your beloved offspring would one day be labeled insane, that he'd be mocked and laughed at, would you still become a parent?

If you knew that no matter how perfect he was, people would daily try to find fault in your child, would you still want to become a parent?

If you knew your child would be arrested for something he didn't do and put on trial with a lineup of false witnesses testifying against him, would you still choose to become a parent?

If you knew your innocent son would be sentenced to an excruciating and humiliating death, would you still want to become a parent?

If you knew that in spite of all the good he had done for others, your child would die naked and friendless, would you still become a parent?

If you knew that because of your son's death someone far less worthy would be able to live, and if you had the power to stop it all, would you?

God knew; he had the power; and he still gave us Jesus.

Thoughts to Ponder

As a father, how do you think God felt, knowing what his Son was going to have to face while on earth?

Why do you think God went ahead and gave his Son, Jesus, to the world?

Bumper Sticker for the Day

> **When it comes to his Son, Jesus,
> God knows how to give 'til it hurts.**

Scripture to Stand On

My God, my God, why have you forsaken me? Why are you so far from saving me, so far from the words of my groaning?

PSALM 22:1

Hello Again, Lord ...

Thank you, Father, for the sacrifice of your Son, which we didn't deserve and too often don't fully appreciate.

4. Pushing Buttons

Have you ever stepped onto an elevator and not really cared where it would take you? Maybe you even pushed all of the buttons and stood there while it opened its door to the second, third, fourth floor, and so on. Most of the floors may even have looked alike, but you didn't care. Without a clear destination in mind, one floor was just as good as the next.

When you know where you're headed, though, it's a different story. You step on to the elevator and confidently push your button. It doesn't matter then whether the fifth floor looks exactly like the seventh floor, you know you're going to be getting off on the seventh. That's the floor you need to be on. Nothing can distract you.

Life can be a lot like riding an elevator. We can have a clear direction for where we're headed. We can push the right button and wait patiently for our floor to come up because we know that's where we're supposed to be—clearly in the center of God's will. Or we can stand on the elevator, aimlessly pushing button after button, waiting for the doors to open to nowhere in particular. Whether we get off on the fourth floor or the fifth doesn't really matter. We're in motion, riding the same elevator as everyone else, but we don't have a clue where we're headed.

Thoughts to Ponder

Do you have a clear direction for where you're headed?

Why do you think it's important to have well-defined goals?

Bumper Sticker for the Day

> **If you don't know where you're going, how will you know when you've missed it?**

Scripture to Stand On

Commit your way to the Lord; trust in him and he will do this.

PSALM 37:5

Hello Again, Lord ...

Lord, show me your will for my life, and grant me the faith to trust you until you do.

5. Run for Cover

Do you know someone who claims to trust God, then runs for cover at the first sight of trouble?

"My faith is in Jesus Christ ... and in this bunker if there's a worldwide computer failure."

"God has promised to never leave me or forsake me, but I think this crisis is more than even he counted on."

"God never fails ... but here's my backup plan just in case."

While proclaiming their trust in our heavenly Father, they're placing their trust in man-made security blankets. Don't get me wrong. There's nothing wrong with preparing for the future, budgeting your time and money so you'll be able to eat as well tomorrow as you're eating today. But if you're depending upon your own ability to survive, rather than on God's ability to take care of you, you could be in for a rude awakening.

Life is unpredictable. Why do you think the cost of insurance is so high? None of us know what tomorrow might bring. We don't know what wonders are in store for us any more than we know what disasters may come our way. We could burglar-proof our home by installing eighteen locks on each door and window, then have to stand by and watch our cherished belongings turn to ash in an unexpected fire. We could move to a secluded, self-sustaining cabin with its own generator and well for water, only to have that seclusion become a curse when a family member needs emergency medical care and none is available.

If we're placing our trust in the things we can do to guarantee our safety, then our trust is misplaced. God is the only one who can truly take care of us. He knows what dangers might cross our path. We have to believe that he will be there for us, no matter what. He's the only security blanket we can truly count on.

Thoughts to Ponder

Do you find yourself placing your trust in what man can do, rather than in what God can do?

When you're facing a problem, what percentage of your trust do you feel you give to God? 100 percent? 70 percent? 40 percent? 10 percent?

Bumper Sticker for the Day

In God we trust.
Everyone else failed the qualification test.

Scripture to Stand On

My help comes from the Lord, the Maker of heaven and earth.

PSALM 121:2

Hello Again, Lord ...

Lord, how can I stand if my plans aren't your plans?

6. Who Are You?

Entertainer Fred Travalena is gifted when it comes to doing impressions. He has mastered the voices and gestures of movie stars, political figures, and just about every other notable person you can think of. When he's doing his impressions, you would almost swear you're in the company of Ronald Reagan, Bill Clinton, Jack Nicholson, Michael Jackson, or whoever else he happens to be imitating.

Fred also has his own voice. He's a nice guy. When I was working on "The Mark & Kathy Show" with Mark Lowry and Kathy Troccoli, Fred was one of our guest stars. Before the show, I enjoyed talking with him about his family, his career, and the state of the entertainment industry today. He was down-to-earth and committed to his craft and his God. Even though his impressions are expertly crafted and hysterically funny, talking to the real Fred Travalena was as enjoyable as watching his performance.

Do you know that sometimes we take on different identities, too? We may do one impression of who we are for our parents, and do another, completely different, impression for our friends. We might even have a third one for our church youth group and a fourth for when we think no one's around who knows us—you know, like when that waiter takes too long to bring us our food or when we're going to places we shouldn't on the Internet.

Doing impressions the way Fred Travalena does them is fun. His talent has helped him make a career out of being other people, and there's nothing wrong with that. We watch him perform and we laugh. That's what we're supposed to do. But Fred knows who the real Fred Travalena is. When he's off the stage, he doesn't have to keep changing who he is to suit the crowd he's with.

Neither do we.

Thoughts to Ponder

Have you ever found yourself taking on a different identity to suit the people you were with?

Why do you think it's important that we be ourselves?

Bumper Sticker for the Day

> **Heaven: No imposters allowed.**

Scripture to Stand On

You know my folly, O God; my guilt is not hidden from you.

PSALM 69:5

Hello Again, Lord ...

Thank you, Lord, that I can be real with you.

7. Unlikely Treasures

Every once in awhile there'll be a story in the news about someone buying a seemingly worthless picture frame at a garage sale, only to find a priceless piece of art hidden behind the cardboard. Or they'll pick up an old knickknack for fifty cents, have it appraised, and discover it's a rare antique worth thousands of dollars.

Most of us miss these great finds because we tend to choose only those items that need the least amount of cleaning up. We pass over the ones that are covered in dust and rust and years of neglect. They require way too much effort. Besides, a treasure would look more like, well, a treasure, wouldn't it?

As a society, we often don't recognize the hidden value of individuals either. That boy, the one who is always getting into trouble, can't possibly be a treasure, can he? After all, just look at all the dirt and scratches on him. He's too much work to be of any real value. So we pass over him and pass up our chances at finding a hidden treasure.

And as for that girl who everyone has always said is no good, maybe we need to take a closer look at her, too. Maybe peek behind that stained and wrinkled cardboard covering. Who knows, we might find a priceless Van Gogh just waiting to be uncovered.

A little dirt—or even a lot of dirt—doesn't change the worth of a diamond. Its value remains intact no matter how it appears on the outside. In the same way, we might discover the hidden treasures in each of us only after we've looked beyond the dust and the layers of life to find them.

Thoughts to Ponder

What do you think might be a hidden treasure in you?

What steps can you take to start uncovering that treasure?

Bumper Sticker for the Day

> **A dusty gem is still a gem.**

Scripture to Stand On

I will sing to the Lord all my life; I will sing praise to my God as long as I live.

PSALM 104:33

Hello Again, Lord ...

Lord, forgive me for burying the treasures you've given to me. Help me to start the excavation process today.

8. Inhibitions

When I'm alone at home, I often lose all inhibitions and do something outrageous. Most of the bottom level of my house has hardwood floors—shiny, smooth hardwood floors. I've discovered that if I get a running start from the carpeted master bedroom and hit the hardwood den floor, I can slide all the way to the kitchen sink before coming to a stop. It's like a Slip 'n Slide without the water.

My family doesn't know I do this. If they did, they'd probably see to it that I got out of the house a little more often. I'm not sure whether my neighbors can see me doing it. I usually keep the blinds closed, and since no one's reported me to the Homeowners' Association yet, I think my secret's safe.

So I keep on doing it. Why? Because it's free, it's harmless (as long as I don't do a somersault over the ottoman and crash into the bookshelf with all the glass picture frames), and it's fun.

Life is a journey. Like any other trip, there will be portions that are exciting, exhilarating, and filled with one Kodak moment after another. There may also be long stretches that are monotonous and downright boring at times.

We each have within us the power to keep life spontaneous. I'm not talking about taking unsafe risks with your health or life (I now move the ottoman out of the way so I won't trip over it), I'm just talking about good, clean fun.

Growing up is something we're all anxious to do, but we need to make sure that as we're growing up, we're not outgrowing our sense of fun in the process.

Thoughts to Ponder

When's the last time you did something outrageous without caring what others thought?

Why do you think it's important to keep a sense of fun as we grow older?

Bumper Sticker for the Day

> **Rapunzel isn't the only one who should get to let her hair down.**

Scripture to Stand On

May my meditation be pleasing to him, as I rejoice in the Lord.

PSALM 104:34

Hello Again, Lord ...

Lord, help me to remember that when I put away childish things, a childlike heart shouldn't be one of them.

9. The Breath of Life

After the doctor told me that my mother had only a few weeks to live, I remember thinking that I wanted to remember what her breath felt like. Her breath would hit my cheek whenever I got close enough, either feeding her or giving her medicine. I didn't know how much longer she would have breath, and I wanted to lock it into my memory.

Contrary to what the doctor had predicted, my mother ended up living another eight months. Those final months were some of the best of my life, which is why I've never understood euthanasia. Aside from the moral issue, euthanasia cheats loved ones out of some wonderful times together. I wouldn't trade those last eight months that I got to spend with my mother for anything.

She knew she had lymphoma, and even though everything was being done to fight it, there was a possibility that she would die. Knowing that, our conversations became more real. No more superficial chitchat about everyday life. She opened up and shared her fears, her feelings, and her memories. It was a privilege to take her for her chemotherapy, blood tests, or blood transfusions. Not knowing when the end might come, I savored every word she spoke.

The end did come. I didn't want it to, but I have some wonderful memories that I otherwise wouldn't have had. And yes, to this day I can still remember the feel of her breath.

Breath is precious, no matter what your stage of life.

Thoughts to Ponder

Why do you think breath is precious to God?

If you were told you had only a short time to live, how would your priorities change?

Bumper Sticker for the Day

Life—a gift that's appreciated more
the less we have left of it.

Scripture to Stand On

Do not cast me away when I am old; do not forsake me when my strength is gone.

PSALM 71:9

Hello Again, Lord ...

Lord, help me to appreciate your breath of life in myself and others.

10. Just Joking

Have you ever played a practical joke on someone only to have it completely backfire in your face? When I was in high school, there was one teacher I especially enjoyed. My Modern Science teacher was so likeable and charismatic, he even got me to memorize the elements chart for him. It hasn't come up in my life since, but I did memorize it.

One day, I thought it would be a great idea to bring a birthday card to class and have all the students sign it for him. It wasn't his birthday, but that was the joke. We'd present him with a birthday card on just an ordinary day. We'd even break out into a few choruses of "Happy Birthday." In my head, the joke was going to be hysterical.

None of the other students, of course, knew that it was a hoax. They signed the birthday card, thinking they were really doing something special.

When it came time to present it, I conned one of the students who had a seat close to the front into handing the teacher the card and leading the rest of us in song. It all went off without a hitch. That is, until the teacher choked up. "No one's ever done anything like this for me before," he said. "It's not my birthday, but this was so thoughtful. I don't think I'll ever forget it." There were tears in his eyes ... and a sick feeling in the pit of my stomach.

My fellow classmates took his reaction exactly as they should have—it was sincere and heartfelt. I was the only one who felt any embarrassment at all.

That's the one thing about practical jokes. They're unpredictable. We never know whether they're going to play out as planned or take an unexpected detour. In my case, the diversion was a positive one. The teacher truly was touched. That's not a bad thing. But in other cases, a practical joke can turn into a hurtful situation. And if there's no laughter involved, it's not a practical joke. It's a practical injury.

Thoughts to Ponder

Have you ever played a practical joke on someone that didn't go off as intended?

Have you ever had a practical joke played on you that wasn't very funny? How did it make you feel?

Bumper Sticker for the Day

> **The best jokes are the ones**
> **at which everyone can laugh.**

Scripture to Stand On

I will behave wisely in a perfect way.

PSALM 101:2, NKJV

Hello Again, Lord ...

Lord, help my laughter not to come at the pain of someone else.

11. Amazing!

If you've sat through very many church services, you've no doubt heard the term "amazing grace." What's so amazing about this thing called "grace," anyway? Why do we preach about it, write songs and books about it, and even tell our friends and family about it? After all, grace is just grace, isn't it?

Well, yes, grace is grace. But *amazing* grace is the kind that God offers us, and that's where the difference comes in.

Amazing grace is being sent to the principal's office for acting up in class and having him not only forgive you, but add your name to the honor roll, too.

Amazing grace is stealing money from your parents so you can go on a two-day shopping spree, then having them throw a party for you when you return.

Amazing grace is taking your neighbor's motorcycle out for a spin without asking, then, when you confess it to him, having him offer to take you out and buy you one of your own.

Amazing grace is unearned favor. It's deserving punishment, but receiving forgiveness *and* favor instead. It's acting like a traitor, but being accepted like a confidant. It's being treated better than you've ever been treated in your life after having acted worse than you've ever acted in your life.

Amazing grace isn't having someone condone your bad behavior. It's having them look beyond it to recognize and reward the good inside you.

Like the song says, it's *amazing*.

Thoughts to Ponder

Why do you think it's impossible to earn God's grace?

If God's grace could be earned, would Jesus have had to die?

Bumper Sticker for the Day

> **The amazing thing about grace is how generous God is with giving it to us and how stingy we are in sharing it with others.**

Scripture to Stand On

I acknowledged my sin to you and did not cover up my iniquity. I said, "I will confess my transgressions to the Lord"—and you forgave the guilt of my sin.

PSALM 32:5

Hello Again, Lord ...

Lord, thank you for loving me when I was unlovable, and for forgiving me when my actions were unforgivable. Thank you for your amazing grace.

12. Shhhh ...

Picture this: you're working on an experiment in science class, and accidentally discover the cure for cancer. Would you pass up the certain "A" and keep the formula a secret so you'd have it all to yourself? Or would you share the good news with your teacher, the media, and every cancer patient you knew?

Or imagine that on a field trip with your history class, you stumble onto a fountain of youth so powerful that after just one drink you're sure to live forever. Would you interrupt the class lecture to tell the others about it, or would you keep quiet and be the only one showing up at your three-hundred-year class reunion?

Now, what if you had a friend who would stand by you when everyone else turned their backs, someone who truly loved his friends unconditionally. Would you introduce him to others, or would you keep his friendship all to yourself?

Jesus is our cure for hopeless situations. Because of his sacrifice on the cross, we've been given the chance for eternal life. He's also a friend who loves unconditionally. So, are you sharing this good news with those around you, or are you keeping it all to yourself?

Jesus—he's one secret we're not supposed to be keeping.

Thoughts to Ponder

God could write the gospel message in the clouds every morning. Why do you think he chooses to have us tell it instead?

Pray for God to lead you to someone this week who needs you to tell him or her about Jesus. Note it here when he does.

Bumper Sticker for the Day

> **The way some of us spread the gospel so sparingly, you'd think it was fattening.**

Scripture to Stand On

I do not hide your righteousness in my heart; I speak of your faithfulness and salvation. I do not conceal your love and your truth from the great assembly.

PSALM 40:10

Hello Again, Lord ...

Lord, I'm thankful that someone shared the gospel with me. May I be just as generous with others.

13. Mercy Me!

One of these days I'm going to get to go see the play *Les Miserables*. I've seen the movie and read the book, and in my opinion it's one of the most beautiful stories of mercy and redemption ever written.

Jean Valjean steals a loaf of bread and is thrown into a French prison. Some nineteen years later, he's released on parole. He's free, but the world isn't very accepting of a man with a past. Taken in by a kind and gentle bishop, Valjean repays the kindness he's been shown by stealing some of the bishop's silver. When the police catch him and bring him back to the bishop, Jean Valjean is certain he's going to be returned to prison. But the bishop tells the police that he gave the silver to Valjean, and then even hands him some candlesticks to go along with it. The bishop's act of mercy turns Valjean's life around.

There are some people, believe it or not, who would argue that the bishop lied to the police when he said he had given Jean Valjean the silver, and since lying is wrong, the bishop had sinned. They miss the whole point of mercy and redemption.

This is similar to how the Pharisees missed the point of the gospel. They got hung up on the law and didn't see that the fulfillment of the law was standing right in front of them. Whenever it comes to erring on the side of law or the side of mercy, err on the side of mercy. That's what the bishop did. That's what Jesus did. That's what we should do, too.

Thoughts to Ponder

If you were in the bishop's position, what would you do?

Why do you think God wants us to show mercy to one another?

Bumper Sticker for the Day

Mercy—a Christian isn't fully dressed without it.

Scripture to Stand On

With the merciful you will show yourself merciful.

PSALM 18:25, NKJV

Hello Again, Lord ...

Lord, may I be generous with my mercy so you'll be generous with yours toward me.

14. Playing With Fire

During one of Southern California's many wildfires, my husband, an officer with the LAPD, was flagged down by a couple of citizens to investigate what looked like a burned mannequin in a field through which the fire had just passed.

It wasn't a mannequin.

A camera was discovered near the body, so it was speculated that the young man, probably in his twenties, was driving by the fire and had decided to stop and take a picture. Evidentally, he tried to get as close as he could without endangering himself. Many fires, though, can travel at incredible speeds and shift direction at a moment's notice. This was one of those fires, and the man paid a heavy price for his curiosity. Within seconds he was totally engulfed in flames and lost his life.

Sometimes we get a little too close to things we know we shouldn't. We're only wanting a better look, or maybe just to feel the rush of excitement for a second or two, then we'll move away to a safer distance. But in an instant, we can get burned.

That premarital sex wasn't supposed to bring along a sexually transmitted disease. That "innocent" gossip wasn't supposed to get back to the people we were talking about and cost us their friendship and trust. Our experimentation with that drug wasn't supposed to leave us dependent upon it.

Fire. It's unpredictable and it burns those who get too close to it. I'm sure that young man had no idea that what he was doing would put his life in jeopardy, but he didn't get a second chance to think it over. By the time he realized he was in danger, it was too late for him to escape.

Thoughts to Ponder

Is there a fire to which you're getting too close?

Why do you think we sometimes don't look at the risks involved with our behavior?

Bumper Sticker for the Day

> **Those who live on the edge
> sometimes fall over.**

Scripture to Stand On

Can a man take fire in his bosom, and his clothes not be burned?

PROVERBS 6:27, KJV

Hello Again, Lord ...

Lord, help me to always keep a safe distance from that which can burn me.

15. Hope Floats ... and Helps

Thankfully, no one I know personally has ever been the victim of a violent crime—murder, armed robbery, rape—although my husband, a twenty-eight-year veteran LAPD sergeant, has had to take plenty of reports on such acts.

Unfortunately, today's society is a violent one. Columbine taught us that tough lesson. And it's not just Columbine. According to statistics, every day some thirteen children are killed at schools across our country. While the reasons behind such insanity can be debated, I believe one cause is a sense of hopelessness that is becoming more and more prevalent. Those committing these acts of violence feel there's no other way to express their anger and sense of despair. They're crying out for help, perhaps have been for months or even years, and we're not hearing them. They're so blinded by their crisis of the moment, they can't see a future, much less let the notion of one guide their decisions. They live hopelessness, breathe hopelessness, and react in hopelessness.

We blame their family life, our schools, and society as a whole, and maybe some of the fault can be placed there. But what about us—you and me? We know the source of hope, have the source of hope, and yet those around us still don't know where to find it. Maybe we're not pointing the way as clearly as we think we are.

Thoughts to Ponder

Is there someone you know who seems to have lost hope?

In what ways could you reach out to this person?

Bumper Sticker for the Day

> **Hope is like oxygen:**
> **we can exist without it, but only for so long.**

Scripture to Stand On

Therefore my heart is glad, and my glory rejoiceth: my flesh also shall rest in hope.

PSALM 16:9, KJV

Hello Again, Lord ...

Lord, may those who need your hope not have to look too hard to see it in me.

16. Close, but ...

When I was writing the parody lyrics for Mark Lowry's version of Ricky Martin's "Livin' La Vida Loca" ("Livin' for Deep-Fried Okra"), I had to make sure every new word matched the original lyric as closely as possible. It had to have the same number of syllables, the accent had to fall in the same place for each word; it needed to sound so much like the Ricky Martin song that the listener wouldn't be able to tell the difference without paying close attention to the lyrics. The project kept me up all night, and for several rewrites afterward, but the end result was, I hope, worth it.

I've written a lot of parodies throughout my writing career, mostly for Mark Lowry and Bob Hope, and it's the same story for all of them. When writing a parody, you've got to get as close to the original as possible.

But parody writers aren't the only ones who try to get as close to the original as possible. So does the enemy. He'll try to trick you into thinking that God said something that he didn't really say or that he didn't say something that he did. How will he do it? By getting as close to the real words as possible. It'll sound almost like the original, but not quite. There'll be just enough truth in it to make you fall for his scam, only to realize later you've been duped. It's not what God said at all. It's a parody.

In other words, it'll be close, but ...

Thoughts to Ponder

Have you ever been tricked by a "parody" of God's Word?

Why is it important to test the things we hear against God's Word?

Bumper Sticker for the Day

God's Word doesn't need a rewrite.

Scripture to Stand On

O my people, hear my teaching; listen to the words of my mouth.

PSALM 78:1

Hello Again, Lord ...

Lord, whenever I'm in doubt, remind me to go to your Word and check it out.

17. Unchained Kindness

There are two types of kindness. One is like a pen at a bank. It looks and feels like a real pen, but if you try to go very far with it, you'll discover it's hooked to the desk by a small but sturdy chain. You're free to use and enjoy it all you want, but only under the bank's scrutiny. Take one step too far with it and it'll snap you back right where they want you.

The other type of kindness doesn't have any chains attached. It's a free pen that's simply given away. The recipient may do whatever he or she wants with it. The pen isn't monitored, nor is it restricted in its uses. It can be truly appreciated, because what you see is what you get—a pen. That's all it is, and that's all you need it to be. It's as simple as that.

The unfortunate thing about the first kind of kindness is that we don't always see the chains. That offer of help may be for all the wrong reasons. It may come at a price we're not prepared or willing to pay.

So feel free to evaluate the "kindness" someone shows you. See if it's attached to anything it shouldn't be. If it's not, accept it. If it is, you may want to leave it at the bank.

Thoughts to Ponder

Have you ever been shown a kindness that had strings attached to it?

What does this say about the true nature of the kindness?

Bumper Sticker for the Day

> **Kindness is like a balloon—**
> **it'll go a lot farther with no strings attached.**

Scripture to Stand On

Do not take away my soul along with sinners or my life with bloodthirsty men, in whose hands are wicked schemes, whose right hands are full of bribes.

PSALM 26:9-10

Hello Again, Lord ...

Lord, help me to recognize when a kindness has no strings attached, and help me to pass along the same.

18. Here I Come to Save the Day

One of my favorite cartoons when I was growing up was Mighty Mouse. Whenever the girl mouse would get into trouble (say, find herself tied to a railroad track or on a conveyor belt headed to a lumber mill and just about to get a mohawk hairdo the hard way), Mighty Mouse would fly down and rescue her, just in the nick of time, singing his famous, "Here I come to save the day!"

Maybe there are times when you feel like Mighty Mouse, when you think it's up to you to "save the day." You're having to straighten out problems here and clean up messes there. It seems as though everyone's happiness and safety is 100 percent dependent upon you, and you're not even sure how much longer you're going to be able to fly.

If you're a child of alcoholic or other substance-abusing parents, you almost certainly feel this way. Maybe you're the one having to excuse their behavior or put them into bed at night. Maybe you've been having to act like the parent for years, and you may not know how much more you can take.

If you're in the middle of divorcing parents, you may think you've got to "fix" whatever problem they are having, too. Maybe you've even convinced yourself that you're the problem. You're not, but your emotions may not let you accept an acquittal. You know your parents are determined to leave each other, so you feel you've got to swoop down and save the day.

Swooping down to "save the day" may work for Mighty Mouse, but it doesn't always work for us in real life. Some problems aren't that easily fixed. Oh, we can try, but often professional intervention is needed. No matter how much we'd like to have the power to change a situation, it's often not up to us.

The ultimate responsibility for change lies within the person or couple involved. A minister, counselor, or other trained individual can help get to the true root of the problem. You can be there for your parents. God can even change their hearts. But it's up to them to call to him from the railroad track.

Thoughts to Ponder

Do you sometimes feel like others expect you to "save the day"?

Do you think it's fair for someone else to expect you to solve all of their problems?

Bumper Sticker for the Day

> **Those who try to carry the world on their shoulders eventually have a hard time standing up themselves.**

Scripture to Stand On

The Lord is their strength, and He is the saving refuge of His anointed.

PSALM 28:8, NKJV

Hello Again, Lord ...

Lord, remind me that "saving the day" is something you're a lot better at than I am.

19. Ask and Ye Shall Receive

I'm amazed at the things I don't ask for. I don't ask for help when I can't see over the stack of packages I'm carrying into the post office, even though I have been trying for five minutes to enter through the brick wall.

I don't ask for help when I'm trying to assemble a 112-piece bicycle which is ending up looking more like a prop for an alien space movie than earthly sports equipment.

I don't ask for help when I'm lost in the mall parking lot, even though it's eleven o'clock at night and the night watchman has driven past me six times in his security cart.

I don't ask for help upgrading my computer. Instead, I keep going to Kinko's and paying twenty cents a minute for the use of theirs.

Other than prayer, there's not a lot that I ask from other people. Maybe I don't want to hear them say no. But those times when I've finally worked up the courage to ask for something, "no" isn't usually the answer I hear. Lately, especially.

"Would you mind picking me up from the airport?"
"Of course not! What time and where?"

"Can you help me with my computer?"
"Sure thing! How about this afternoon?"

"Would you mind dropping this off at the post office?"
"Not at all. I'd be happy to."

For the most part, I've found that people are ready, willing, and to my surprise, eager to help. I'd never have known that, though, if I hadn't started asking, if I had continued doing everything myself.

Maybe that's why the Lord tells us to "ask and ye shall receive." Maybe he's just waiting to show us how willing he is to help us out.

Thoughts to Ponder

Is there something you need that you haven't talked to God about yet?

What do you think is keeping you from asking?

Bumper Sticker for the Day

> **Ask and you shall receive.**
> **Keep silent and you shall always wonder.**

Scripture to Stand On

You have granted him the desire of his heart and have not withheld the request of his lips.

PSALM 21:2

Hello Again, Lord ...

Lord, give me boldness when I need to speak up and patience when I need to hush up.

20. Puzzle Pieces

One of my favorite computer games is Tetris. I'm sure most of you have played it, but, for those who haven't, the object of the game is to fit as many puzzle pieces together to make as many lines as fast as you can. It's a fun game and requires concentration and skill.

Life gives us a lot of puzzle pieces to put together, too. Sometimes those pieces fit together easily; other times we have to work a little harder at it. Once in a while, we even get stuck with a piece that doesn't fit, no matter how hard we work at it. We end up wanting to erase that game and start over with a new set of puzzle pieces.

Life isn't Tetris, however, and we don't get to start over. We just have to trust that the puzzle pieces we've been given will eventually fit together and make sense. Maybe not today. Perhaps not even tomorrow. It may not even be until we reach heaven, but one day the pieces will fit together perfectly and we'll know that everything—the good, the bad, the frustrating, the confusing, the disappointing, the surprising, the embarrassing, the funny, the serious—all served a purpose in our lives.

Thoughts to Ponder

Are there some puzzle pieces in your life that you just can't seem to fit together?

What should you do when life hands you a puzzle piece that doesn't make any sense right now?

Bumper Sticker for the Day

A puzzle needs all the pieces to be complete.

Scripture to Stand On

The Lord will perfect that which concerns me.

PSALM 138:8, KJV

Hello Again, Lord ...

Lord, help me to trust you when life gets puzzling.

21. A Tale of Two Voices

A boxer has two voices he can listen to. One is the voice of his trainer. It'll be saying positive things like, "You can do it!" "You're the champ!" "Don't give up now!" "Just one more round!" The other voice is that of his opponent. His comments aren't usually quite so encouraging: "You call that a punch?" "What a loser!" "Throw in the towel! It's over!" The outcome of the fight can often depend on which voice the boxer chooses to heed.

You'll hear two kinds of voices as you go through life, too. One kind will keep pushing you on, convincing you to hang in there or to get back up on your feet after you've been knocked down. The other will be the voices of discouragement. They'll tell you that you can't do it. They'll try to convince you to throw in the towel and get out of the ring. They'll tell you it's over. It doesn't take a rocket scientist to know which voice is the one coming from a godly place.

Just as the boxer must determine which voice he's going to listen to, so must we. We can either take the encouragement to heart and keep going to a knockout, or we can listen to the discouragement, give in, and surrender the championship belt.

Thoughts to Ponder

What kind of voices do you tend to listen to more often—encouraging or discouraging?

What do you think the motive is behind discouraging voices?

Bumper Sticker for the Day

> **Encouragement—**
> **one gift no one ever returns to the store.**

Scripture to Stand On

For surely, O Lord, you bless the righteous; you surround them with your favor as with a shield.

PSALM 5:12

Hello Again, Lord ...

Lord, help me to hear the words I should hear and ignore the ones I should ignore.

22. For Crying Out Loud

Do you know God sees you when you cry? You may be all alone in your room, thinking no one cares or even knows you're hurting, but God does. He sees every tear you shed and even the oceans of tears you feel like crying. He knows when you're hurting and he knows exactly what it is that's bothering you. You don't even have to tell him about it, although he's ready and eager to listen whenever you want to talk it over with him.

Whatever it is you may be dealing with, don't be afraid to be vulnerable with God. Your tears matter to him, so much that he even keeps track of them. That's how David was able to survive those years when he was being unjustly pursued. According to Psalms, David shed more than his share of tears. But he knew that God was counting those tears, and that one day a smile would return to his face.

God's counting your tears, too, and one day your smile will return ... just like David's did.

Thoughts to Ponder

How does it make you feel to know that God keeps track of your tears?

Have you talked your situation over with God? With your parents? With a counselor?

Bumper Sticker for the Day

Sometimes we see better after our eyes
have been washed with tears.

Scripture to Stand On

Record my lament; list my tears on your scroll—are they not in your record?

PSALM 56:8

Hello Again, Lord ...

Lord, thank you that not a single tear has fallen from my eyes without you knowing it.

23. www.creation.com

Now that we're on this side of Y2K, we know that the world hasn't come to an end, as some tried to make us believe it would. Not that the world as we know it isn't going to come to an end someday. The Bible clearly states that it will. But it won't be on a day that man has predicted. It will be on a day that God, and God alone, has set aside.

God didn't need a computer to create the world. He didn't type in "www.creation.com" and let Bill Gates handle the job. God's own hands formed the mountains and scooped out the seas. Genesis doesn't mention one word about God needing a Microsoft program to do his work. The earth and all that is in it is a result of his plan and power, not a website designer.

Throughout your life, you're sure to hear your share of doomsday predictions. My family and friends believe that my cooking will bring about the demise of civilization as we know it, but that hasn't happened yet, either. The simple truth is that none of us know what God will use to usher in the last days, but one thing's for certain: whatever it is, he will be the one in charge. Nothing is going to happen in this world that will catch him off guard.

So keep your trust where it should be: In him, not in your PC, your Mac, or any other thing that you've come to depend on. God's the same yesterday, today, and after Y2K.

Thoughts to Ponder

Why do you think it's important to keep a level head at all times?

Which do you think God wants us to do—run in fear or live in faith?

Bumper Sticker for the Day

> **Aside from their first letter,**
> **fear and faith don't have a lot in common.**

Scripture to Stand On

My mouth will tell of your righteousness, of your salvation all day long, though I know not its measure.

PSALM 71:15

Hello Again, Lord ...

Lord, help me not to run in fear when I should be standing in faith.

24. A Mouthful of Problems

We've all said things we wish we hadn't said. Like the time I tried to compliment a lady who had lost about ten pounds. She was petite to begin with, but the loss of those ten pounds really did look good on her. Instead of simply saying she looked great, though, I had to go a step further. I had to REALLY compliment her.

"You look terrific!" I said, bubbling with sincere enthusiasm. "You've lost a TON of weight!"

It had sounded a lot more complimentary in my head. There was an uncomfortable silence, and then I did my best to try to talk my way out of it. I explained what I had meant, as opposed to what had come out of my mouth, but the more I talked, the worse I felt.

They say when you dig yourself into a hole, sometimes the best thing to do is just stop digging. Good advice. I try to do the three A's and get out. The first A is to *acknowledge* the fact that there is a hole and that you are indeed in that hole. Pretending the hole doesn't exist or that you had nothing to do with it only makes matters worse.

The next A is *apologize*. Apologizing is something you do as much for yourself as for the other person. And it needs to be a real apology. Admit that what you said could easily have been taken wrong, and that the other party has every right to be offended. If you're being honest, and you don't have a history of being hurtful, he or she will probably accept your apology. Luckily, in my case, the lady did.

The last A is to do an *about-face*. Don't just sit there wallowing in the situation. Learn from it, so that next time you won't be so quick to say or do something that you'll later regret. After all, when God told us to live holy lives, digging holes with our words or our actions wasn't what he meant.

Thoughts to Ponder

Have you ever found yourself at the bottom of a hole that you dug yourself?

Did you try to explain your intentions to the other person? What was the result?

Bumper Sticker for the Day

> **Make sure the words you say are ones you're not going to mind eating.**

Scripture to Stand On

I said, "I will watch my ways and keep my tongue from sin."
PSALM 39:1

Hello Again, Lord ...

Lord, help me to remember that you put our brains on top, above our mouths. You meant for them to be used in that order.

25. What's All the Growling About?

Once, while on a camping trip with my family, I learned a good lesson about worry. First of all, I should say I'm not the camping type. I prefer a nice, warm hotel room with room service. I'm not all that fond of sharing my sleeping bag with a raccoon, no matter how polite he is.

On this particular camping trip, I stayed awake most of the night, keeping vigil, because the zipper on our tent had broken and we had only a few safety pins keeping the wild critters out. I knew there were plenty of them out there, because throughout the night I could hear them scratching on the side of the canvas. There was one critter, though, I hadn't counted on hearing from. A lion. Not a mountain lion. Not an alley cat with an attitude problem. A real lion!

"Did you hear that?!" I gasped, shaking my husband awake.

"Hear what?" he said, grumpily.

"That!" There it was again. "There's a lion outside our tent!"

He peered at me through half-open eyes. "Right," he said, before rolling over and going back to sleep.

His snoring didn't stop the growling. It made it more difficult to hear, but it was still there. Once again, I shook him awake.

"What is it?!" he demanded.

"The lion. He's still out there."

"Then stick another safety pin in the tent and go back to sleep. We'll talk about it in the morning."

In the morning! The whole family would be Lion Chow by then, I thought to myself. It was now up to me to keep watch, to make sure no lion paws tried to reach in and snatch our offspring in the middle of the night. I grabbed a frying pan and nestled in my blanket at the edge of the tent, ready to whack the first hairy thing that tried to enter.

Nothing did. By morning I was exhausted, but I was determined to get to the bottom of the mystery. I didn't, however, want to look like a complete idiot, so I was careful when I approached the campground manager about it. "Uh ... did you happen to hear any strange noises last night?"

"Strange?" he asked, matter-of-factly. "What kind of strange?"

"Well, sort of like ... well, you know ... like growling?"

"You mean the lions?" he said.

"Lions?" I asked, emphasizing the plural, and shooting my husband a look of self-vindication.

"There's a wild animal compound up the road a piece. They rent out animals to the movies. They're caged, though. Can't hurt you."

Lion *actors*? I had stayed awake all night for lion *actors*? I felt a little foolish after discovering the truth of the situation, but that's not the first time I've lost sleep worrying over something I didn't need to worry about. I've tossed and turned over things that never happened, or even came close to happening. In other words, the growling we hear in our heads is usually a lot worse than the actual bite.

Thoughts to Ponder

Have you ever stayed awake at night worrying over something?

What should you have been doing instead of worrying?

Bumper Sticker for the Day

> **Worry: Faith on hiatus.**

Scripture to Stand On

If you make the Most High your dwelling ... then no harm will befall you.

PSALM 91:9-10

Hello Again, Lord ...

Lord, with you I never have to fear, no matter how much growling I hear.

26. Keep On Truckin'

My cousin, Ernie Stevens, drives a truck for a living. I admire truck drivers. It has to be grueling trying to stay awake during those long stretches of interstate travel. Maintaining control of the load at all times can get a bit tricky, too. If the load's too heavy, the truck could have difficulty manuevering around sharp corners and up steep hills. If it's too light, the wind could whip the truck out of control.

God knows we need balance with whatever load we're carrying in life, too. If it's too heavy, it can keep us from moving forward at the rate we need to be moving. In a worst-case scenario, it could leave us stranded by the side of the road. If it's too light, though, we could find ourselves swerving in the face of the slightest wind.

God has promised not to give us any more than we can bear. But no problems, no troubles, no load of any kind isn't in our best interest, either. We need a load that is perfectly balanced: not so heavy that it hinders our progress, but just enough to keep us on track and make us arrive at our destination with our faith intact.

Thoughts to Ponder

Have you ever felt like God has given you more than you can bear?

In what ways has God's grace helped you to get through it?

Bumper Sticker for the Day

> **When the going gets tough,
> God's grace is enough.**

Scripture to Stand On

The Lord is my strength and my song; he has become my salvation.

PSALM 118:14

Hello Again, Lord ...

Lord, thank you for always carrying the heaviest portion of the load.

27. Impressed Yet?

Do you know our talents don't impress God? Why would the author of the hottest selling book in the history of literature be overwhelmed by any poem, song, article, or novel that we happen to scribble down?

How could someone who is serenaded daily by choirs of perfect-pitched angels be impressed by our meager voices, no matter how many earthly standing ovations we may receive? My voice could curl the pages of a hymnal, which could be why our music director issued me the only choir robe that came with a gag. So I know I'm not impressing anyone with my singing talent, least of all God.

Do we really think the Inventor of music is going to be impressed by the way we play the piano, drums, trumpet, violin, or any other instrument?

Too often we think we're doing God a favor by offering our talents, whatever they happen to be, to his service. We wrestle with ourselves over the matter, even seek counseling and prayer, then finally give up and agree to dedicate our gift to him as though it's some great sacrifice.

Don't get me wrong. It's commendable to use whatever talents the Lord has given us for his glory, but not because they're so awe-inspiring to him. The Creator of the universe is looking for obedient children, not a great concert to attend on Friday night or a good book to curl up with this weekend. He doesn't *need* our gifts, but he has promised to bless them if we're willing to place them in his hands. And you know what? The amazing thing is, in the balance of his hands, everyone's talents weigh the same.

Thoughts to Ponder

What talents do you feel you have to offer to the Lord?

Why do you think God is more impressed with our obedience than with our talents?

Bumper Sticker for the Day

When's the last time God got a standing ovation?

Scripture to Stand On

Praise the Lord, O my soul. O Lord my God, you are very great; you are clothed with splendor and majesty. He wraps himself in light as with a garment; he stretches out the heavens like a tent and lays the beams of his upper chambers on their waters. He makes the clouds his chariot and rides on the wings of the wind.

PSALM 104:1-3

Hello Again, Lord ...

Lord, help me to do my best for you, but never to confuse my best with yours.

28. Bittersweet

How do you get rid of a bitter taste in your mouth? That's a question often asked by my dinner guests. The answer? Eat something sweet. The sweetness will make your taste buds forget all about the bitter, and the sooner you do it, the sooner the awful taste will go away.

This rule, though, doesn't apply just to food. It applies to life. When something happens that leaves you with a bitter taste, the best way to remedy the situation is to replace that bitterness with something sweet. In other words, replace a bad memory with a good one, a sad recollection with a joyful realization. If a friend has betrayed you, think about all your friends who haven't. Number one on that list should be Jesus. If someone made a cruel remark to you, think about all the positive, encouraging remarks you've been given over the years. If you can't recall any, then take a few moments to read some from the Bible. It's full of them. No matter how bitter the memory, its awful taste will go away as soon as you counter it with something sweet.

So, don't be like my dinner guests and just sit there and complain. There are lots of different items on the table. If you don't like the one you're chewing now, bite into a new taste today.

Thoughts to Ponder

Do you have some bittersweet memories that need replacing?

Why do you think God wants us to guard our hearts against bitterness?

Bumper Sticker for the Day

> A grudge, if stored too long,
> will eventually spoil everything around it.

Scripture to Stand On

How good it is to sing praises to our God, how pleasant and fitting to praise him!

PSALM 147:1

Hello Again, Lord ...

Lord, help me to remember that a grudge has no nutritional value and that I should chew on something else.

29. Tough Guy

It was interesting to watch. The entire evening, all he did was talk about how tough he was—how he had beaten up this person or that person, told this lady off, put that man in his place. He even reenacted some of his more noteworthy confrontations. Clearly, he wanted to convey the fact that he was not someone to be messed with, but his foul-mouthed, chain-smoking bravado made it seem as though he was really a scared little boy. I wondered what he was afraid of. What was it in his life that he so feared facing? Who had bullied him so much that he felt he had to bully others to make up for it?

I've seen some girls act this same way, covering up their fears with a performance so hard-edged as to guarantee no one would dare get close enough to find out who they really were.

Usually it works. Most people honor that invisible barrier and don't even attempt to get to know the actor behind the act. Oh, they may laugh at their stories, or cheer them on as they're downing one drink after another, but they'll keep their distance.

Jesus is a friend, though, who won't keep a "distance." When the five-times-married woman at the well was wanting to just get her water and return home to another man who wasn't her husband, Jesus saw through her act. He knew she was searching for love, real love, but had been looking in all the wrong places. He offered her his "living water," and let her know that she didn't need to keep up her performance with him. He knew everything about her and still loved her. She could let down her guard and be herself with him.

We can, too.

Thoughts to Ponder

Do you, or someone you know, feel a need to hide behind bravado?

Why do you think Jesus wants us to be real with him?

Bumper Sticker for the Day

> **Acting tough doesn't impress Jesus.**
> **Being real does.**

Scripture to Stand On

Be merciful to me, Lord, for I am faint.

PSALM 6:2

Hello Again, Lord ...

Lord, thank you that I can be myself with you.

30. No Guarantees

There are a lot of things in life that come with a guarantee. If you buy a new car one day, it will come with a guarantee not to leave you stranded ... for a few thousand miles at least. That computer you're working on either at your home or at school came with a guarantee to work properly, too. And if your new surfboard sinks to the bottom of the Pacific Ocean, your guarantee tells you that you have a right to complain to the manufacturer (once you swim back up to the surface, that is). Surfboards are, or at least should be, guaranteed to float.

What doesn't come with a guarantee, though, is life. There's nothing written on our birth certificates that guarantees us an easy, carefree journey. We're not even guaranteed long lives. The only thing we're guaranteed is that we have a certain amount of days allotted to us. We don't know how many, but we obviously have some because we're still here.

How we live out those days is up to us. If we don't get enough enjoyment out of them, we can't go back to our Maker and demand a refund. If we fail to accomplish all that we wanted to accomplish, we can't put in a request for an extension. Well, we can, but we have no guarantee that we'll be granted it.

If we live a life that's unsatisfying, unhappy, and unfulfilling, we've no one to blame but ourselves. The potential was there. We just wasted it.

Thoughts to Ponder

Do you feel you appreciate your life as much as you should?

Is there something that you could be doing to make better use of your time here on earth?

Bumper Sticker for the Day

Life is like a movie—
if you're not paying good attention,
you could miss out on some of the best parts.

Scripture to Stand On

Even when I am old and gray,
do not forsake me, O God,
till I declare your power to the next generation,
your might to all who are to come.

PSALM 71:18

Hello Again, Lord ...

Lord, help me to remember that I'm going to get out of life whatever I put into it.

31. Good Night

Have you ever had a night where you just couldn't sleep? I'm not talking about being at a sleepover with your friends or at a youth camp when all the laughter and joking around was keeping you awake. I'm talking about being alone in your bed, just staring at the ceiling. One o'clock, two o'clock, even three o'clock rolls around and you're not even tired. You lie there thinking about everything—like that test you're going to have to take in a few hours and that girl who made that rude remark to you. You wonder what she meant by it, you wonder what you're going to major in at college, you worry about the high cost of gasoline, and you wonder whether the stock market is going to crash. Your mind is going in a million different directions and there's not a thing you can do to shut it off. So you just lie there and count the ceiling tiles—after all, that doesn't really take much concentration.

Do you know that God is concerned that we get the rest we need? He created our bodies, so he knows they require sleep. He even made sure he gave himself ample rest after creating the world.

So the next time you're having trouble sleeping, don't just lie there. Try reading your Bible. Especially Psalms. There are lots of soothing passages in Psalms that will help to take your mind off your troubles. You might even want to be like David and write a few songs of praise yourself. But when you're done, turn out your light and try to get some rest. God thinks it's important. So should you.

Thoughts to Ponder

Do you think you get enough rest for your body?

Why do you think getting your rest is important?

Bumper Sticker for the Day

> **Get plenty of sleep—but getting it in English class could get you suspended.**

Scripture to Stand On

In vain you rise early and stay up late, toiling for food to eat—for he grants sleep to those he loves.

PSALM 127:2

Hello Again, Lord ...

Lord, help me to remember to give my body the rest it needs.

32. Who Are We Waiting For?

Have you ever wondered why God, who has all the resources in the world, would let a child go hungry? Or why he doesn't see to it that every city, town, or village in the world has a church or full-time missionary? He has the money. He could easily part the Red Sea of red tape and make sure the right funds get to the right people so they can be sent to the right places.

So why doesn't he? Why doesn't he see to it that all the benevolent things that need to get done in our society get done? Why should that be a problem we have to deal with? After all, he's the one who owns the cattle on a thousand hills, right? Most of us don't even own one cow and sometimes have to scrape our funds together just to get a single hamburger.

So, where is God when all the suffering of the world is taking place? Maybe he's wondering the same thing about us. Maybe he's wondering how we can sit by and watch children starve. He's wondering how long it's going to take us to help build that church in some foreign country or support a missionary who's already gone there.

God already knows what it feels like to give sacrificially to others. Maybe he wants us to know that feeling, too.

Thoughts to Ponder

Is there a ministry (prison, world hunger, orphanage, etc.) to which you feel particularly drawn?

In what ways can you begin to help out in that particular field of ministry?

Bumper Sticker for the Day

> **The world can change for the better
> as easily as it can for the worse.**

Scripture to Stand On

I will sing of the Lord's great love forever; with my mouth
will I make your faithfulness known through all generations.

PSALM 89:1

Hello Again, Lord ...

Lord, when it comes to helping others, don't let us leave all the
hard work to you.

33. Neighborly Love

No way! There's no way I'm living next to them! If I have to, I'll build a twenty-foot wall between us! No, make that thirty! If they're gonna be our neighbors, we're moving!"

We don't always get along with everyone here on earth, do we? But no matter how much we dislike someone, the above comments are something we're never going to hear in heaven. So why do we live and treat our fellow man as though we'll have the option to ignore him in the hereafter? If both of us make it to the city of gold, chances are we're going to run into each other. And if God has any sense of humor at all—and he does— our mansion just might be the one next door to theirs. And there won't be any relocation experts assigned to the heavenly real estate.

That doesn't mean we have to enjoy being around difficult people, respect them, or allow them to zap our joy. But we do need to get along, especially when they're Christians. The marriage supper of the Lamb isn't going to be any place for a food fight, and crossing to the other side of the golden streets to avoid someone isn't proper afterlife behavior, either.

So no matter how many difficult people you have in your life, try your best to remain at peace with them. You might just have to spend eternity saying, "Howdy, neighbor!"

Thoughts to Ponder

Is there someone you'd hate to have to live next door to throughout eternity?

Why do you think it's a good idea to learn to get along on this side of heaven first?

Bumper Sticker for the Day

> **Love thy neighbor as thyself ...**
> **you may be getting on his nerves, too.**

Scripture to Stand On

How good and pleasant it is when brothers live together in unity!

PSALM 133:1

Hello Again, Lord ...

Lord, help me with the difficult people in my life, because they just might be there in my afterlife, too.

34. What a Delight!

Do you know God delights in you? That's pretty awesome when you think about it. The God who created the universe and everything in it delights in you. Oh, sure, you knew he loved you—after all, he sacrificed his Son for you. You knew he cares about your well-being because the Bible tells you that he does. But you probably didn't realize he delights in you.

We all have friends, but there are some friends we just enjoy being with more than others. Maybe it's because we laugh more when we're with them or we have more adventures. That's the kind of friend we are to God. He delights in being with us. Think about that the next time you're making him wait to spend time with you. Prayer and Bible study aren't just for you, you know. They're an opportunity for God to spend time with you. He looks forward to that. He enjoys it. You're his delight.

Thoughts to Ponder

Did you realize that you were this special to God?

In what ways can you show God that you delight in him, too?

Bumper Sticker for the Day

> **Make a date with God.**
> **He'll never stand you up.**

Scripture to Stand On

He brought me out into a spacious place; he rescued me because he delighted in me.

PSALM 18:19

Hello Again, Lord ...

Lord, forgive me for all those times I've stood you up. How about if we spend some time together right now?

35. Firsthand

You're at a dinner honoring the Lifeguard of the Year. Two speakers are scheduled to talk about the honoree. The first speaker is someone who knows almost everything there is to know about him. He grew up with this guy, went to college with him, and now even works with him. He closes his tribute with the assurance that he would trust this lifeguard with his own life.

The second speaker is a near-drowning victim who was rescued by the honoree. She doesn't know everything there is to know about this lifeguard, but she knows she owes her life to him. If it hadn't been for him, she wouldn't be alive. She's living proof that this lifeguard is everything his resume says he is. For the rest of her life, no matter what anyone else says, her faith in this lifeguard's abilities will never be shaken.

Of the two speakers, whose tribute would be the most convincing?

When we go through difficult times in our lives, we often wonder, "Why me?" Maybe it's so that our knowledge of who God is will become a firsthand experience. Then, when we tell others about him, it'll be a testimonial that people will listen to, relate to, and believe.

Thoughts to Ponder

Have you ever wondered why you have had to deal with a certain problem in your life?

Do you think that your experience could someday help others come to know the Lord?

Bumper Sticker for the Day

> **If we never had a storm,
> we wouldn't need a lighthouse.**

Scripture to Stand On

He lifted me out of the slimy pit, out of the mud and mire;
he set my feet on a rock and gave me a firm place to stand.
He put a new song in my mouth, a hymn of praise to our
God. Many will see and fear and put their trust in the Lord.

PSALM 40:2-3

Hello Again, Lord ...

Lord, when life doesn't make sense—and sometimes it
doesn't—thank you for the lessons I can learn from it. The most
important one is trusting you.

36. All Lit Up

In the town where I live, residents love to decorate for the Christmas holidays. Almost every house is adorned with lights, garlands, wreaths, bells, or a combination of all of the above.

One home in particular is lit up so brightly that it looks like a substation for the electric company. Just about every square inch of the impressive grounds is outlined in twinkling lights. There's even a decorated train sitting on the lawn. It's something to see. Obviously, the owner has spared no expense in showing off his holiday spirit, and the number of cars that slow to a crawl as they drive by prove his annual efforts are appreciated.

Just down the street a bit is another home, with a large open field, complete with barn. On the roof of the barn, the owners have painted the star of Bethlehem. It's a subdued scene, with only one lone spotlight illuminating it, but it catches your eye every bit as much as the other home does. In fact, the contrast between the two homes is quite remarkable.

Now, I'll be the first to admit I love driving around looking at Christmas decorations, and there's absolutely nothing wrong with going a bit overboard with them. After all, this is a holiday where we should be expressing our joy for everything Christmas means to us. But to me, the two homes represent what it must have been like in Bethlehem some two thousand years ago. While everyone's attention was focused on the hustle, bustle, and excitement of the crowded city, who was noticing that one lone star shining softly over the stable where baby Jesus had been born? The answer is simple: those who were looking for it.

Thoughts to Ponder

What's a good way to keep Jesus at the center of your Christmas?

How do you think Jesus feels when he's so often left out of his own birthday celebration?

Bumper Sticker for the Day

> **Jesus—the best gift to share year-round.**

Scripture to Stand On

Be still, and know that I am God; I will be exalted among the nations, I will be exalted in the earth.

PSALM 46:10

Hello Again, Lord ...

Lord, however we celebrate it, may we never forget that you are the star of Christmas.

37. Singing a New Song

The book of Psalms is about singing praises to God. Singing has never been one of my talents. I enjoy writing songs, the words anyway, but I don't sing. Even in church I usually just lip-sync, Milli Vanilli style.

Evidently, though, David could sing. He wrote most of the psalms and even played along on his harp. His songs brought him comfort in his time of despair. Music has a way of doing that. It can lift us up when we're feeling at our lowest. When life has just dealt us another unfair blow, we can find solace in singing praise songs. We can find peace, joy, and renewed strength. Music is powerful.

God understood the power of music. That's why he included this book of Psalms in his Word. It stands out from the other books in the Bible. In fact, Psalms is where you'll find the shortest chapter in the Bible, Psalm 117. There are only two verses in this psalm. I guess that's so you can save your energy for Psalm 119, the longest chapter in the Bible.

So the next time you're feeling down, instead of reaching for the remote control, reach for the book of Psalms. It'll leave you with a song in your heart, and that's a lot better than what you'll get from the evening news.

Thoughts to Ponder

Do you have a favorite psalm?

Why do you think music is important to God?

Bumper Sticker for the Day

> **A song in your heart helps
> drown out the sour notes of life.**

Scripture to Stand On

Sing to him a new song.

PSALM 33:3

Hello Again, Lord ...

Lord, thank you for the song in my heart ... no matter how it
sounds when it comes out.

38. Pleasing Everyone

As soon as the words left my mouth, I wondered why I had said them. I had taken the time to arrive at the airport early, wait in the long check-in line, and change my seat assignment from a window to an aisle seat. Obviously, sitting in an aisle seat was important to me.

But now, after having just settled comfortably into my new seat, there they were—a man, his wife, and their young son—standing over me, asking if I'd mind switching seats so they could sit together. The airline, apparently, had seated the wife and young boy in my row, but the husband's seat was behind us.

"You can sit there," the wife said, pointing to the window seat behind us. "Do you mind?" Her accent was so thick I could barely understand her. I looked at her husband and son, standing next to her looking ever-so-pitiful. How could I even think of splitting up a family?

"It's OK?" she pressed.

"Sure!" I said, convincingly. "Of course, it's OK!"

I sprang to my feet and moved to the window seat behind me, climbing over several pairs of knees in the process. I was now stuck in a window seat, exactly where I didn't want to be. But if I had said no, the entire plane would have thought I was the meanest person alive. Giving up my seat was the right thing to do.

But what happened next taught me a good lesson, too. After only a half hour or so, the man got up and changed his seat, because, as he put it, it was too "squishy" sitting there with his family. So, there I was, stuck in a window seat, feeling cramped and uncomfortable, while this man for whom I had sacrificed didn't think twice about my "gift." He found another seat. Even his wife didn't seem to care, at this point, that he wasn't sitting with the family.

What had happened? Why had it been so important for them to sit together before the plane took off, if it was so unimportant now? I could have gotten up and taken my seat back, but I would have had to climb over all those knees again. I didn't want to make a scene, so I decided to stay where I was and chalk it up to having learned another good lesson in life.

There will be times in our lives when we're asked to give up something that's a whole lot more significant than an airplane seat. In those instances, we need to remember that it's all right to say no. Giving up an airplane seat won't have a lasting impact on my life. Other sacrifices will—especially if they involve giving in to sin.

So the next time anyone—girl, boy, man, or woman—asks you to give up something that's special to you, something that God wouldn't want you to give up, remember that family on the airplane. Your sacrifice may be treated just as flippantly. You may find your gift being tossed aside, leaving you stuck in a place you never wanted to be.

Thoughts to Ponder

Has anyone ever asked you to give up something that was special to you?

Why do you think it's important to stand up for ourselves and God's will for our lives in instances such as these?

Bumper Sticker for the Day

Be careful what you give away—
you may want it back someday.

Scripture to Stand On

It is better to take refuge in the Lord than to trust in man.

PSALM 118:8

Hello Again, Lord ...

Lord, help me to appreciate what I have before it's gone.

39. Full Commitment

A good friend of mine, Tara Leigh Cobble, recently forwarded to me the following e-mail that has been making the rounds. I don't think it's true, but it does give us food for thought. It seems that on a Sunday morning during a worship service, two men covered from head to toe in black and carrying submachine guns entered a two-thousand-member church. One of the men proclaimed, "Anyone willing to take a bullet for Christ, remain where you are."

Immediately, the choir, the deacons, and most of the congregation fled. Of the two thousand who originally occupied the pews, only about twenty remained. The man who had spoken took off his hood and said, "OK, Pastor, I got rid of all the hypocrites. Now you may begin your service. Have a nice day!" Then the two men turned and walked out.

Being willing to die for our faith isn't easy. We're pretty sure, if it came down to it, we'd never deny Christ. But most of us hope our "test" will take place in gym class or at the mall—you know, where there aren't any submachine guns or guillotines around.

The more probing question, though, is this. If a man—dirty, smelly, hair unkempt, guilty of every sin imaginable, living off the streets—were to walk into church one day, who among us would be willing to lay down our lives for him?

By laying down our lives, I mean living our faith, minute by minute, reaching out to those who are badly in need of a friend. By putting that other person's needs ahead of our own. By demonstrating God's love through our hands and hearts.

Our willingness to lay down our lives for Christ is a measure of how serious we are about Christianity. Our willingness to serve a totally unworthy stranger is a measure of how serious we are about becoming more like Christ.

Thoughts to Ponder

How far would you be willing to go in standing up for your faith?

How far would you be willing to go for those who don't know God?

Bumper Sticker for the Day

Those who don't think the cross is heavy
are probably just looking at it, instead of carrying it.

Scripture to Stand On

For you, O God, tested us; you refined us like silver.

PSALM 66:10

Hello Again, Lord ...

Lord, thank you that your love was more than talk.

40. What's the Difference?

When it comes to chicken and fish, there's a lot of difference. Maybe it's not that easy to tell them apart with my cooking (one smoldering entree is as good as another), but there is a difference. Fish has small bones and perhaps even a tail. If you find a tail on a plate of chicken, I'd suggest sending it back.

There are also differences between a football game and a tennis match. First of all, the gear is different. And if you try tackling your opponent in tennis, you won't get cheers. You'll get arrested for assault and battery.

One area, though, where you won't find a lot of difference is sin. We may try to make distinctions. We have our favorites to preach against—adultery, fornication, murder, stealing. But other sins, equal in God's eyes—like pride, greed, and selfishness—are often overlooked.

Yet sin is sin. God doesn't make distinctions, so why do we? If we try to separate sin, like eggs, into neat little baskets of jumbo, medium, and small, we'll end up with a scrambled mess, and an awful lot of egg on our faces.

Thoughts to Ponder

Do you find yourself categorizing sin?

Why do you think God looks at all sin equally?

Bumper Sticker for the Day

> **My sin doesn't look any better than yours,
> no matter how much I dress it up.**

Scripture to Stand On

You have laid down precepts that are to be fully obeyed.

PSALM 119:4

Hello Again, Lord ...

Lord, when I start to elevate my sin above someone else's, remind me that it all looks the same in your eyes.

41. Name-Dropping

I have a friend who name drops every chance she gets. Whenever she can work a celebrity or politician into a conversation, she does. Never mind that she's never met them, or that she knows nothing more about them than what she reads in the tabloids or sees on the Sunday morning political shows. She talks about them as though she's been named in their wills.

Name-dropping is something you do to make people think you're connected. If you can attach your own name to that of someone more important, then it somehow validates you. It makes you seem important, too. After all, if a famous person knows your name, you must be pretty special.

There's one name, though, that we should all be dropping. He's not a movie star, or a senator, or even the president. He's the God of the universe and he counts us among his inner circle of friends. That's quite an honor. You can't get any more connected than that. So, the next time you feel like name-dropping, drop a few of God's names—Lord, Father, Almighty King. It'll really impress your friends.

Thoughts to Ponder

How does it feel to know that God knows who you are?

Do you think you drop his name often enough?

Bumper Sticker for the Day

> It's not who you know. It's Who you know.

Scripture to Stand On

Glory in his holy name; let the hearts of those who seek the
Lord rejoice.

PSALM 105:3

Hello Again, Lord ...

Lord, may our names forever be linked.

42. I'm So Happy I Could Cry

Isn't it aggravating when someone who clearly doesn't deserve good fortune gets it? That girl who always came late to softball practice is suddenly made pitcher. That boy whose father wrote his English essay for him not only gets an "A," but enters the report in a state writing competition and wins that, too. It's hard to act pleased when someone is promoted unfairly or is given credit where credit isn't due. We smile for them, maybe even get out the word "Congratulations," but inside we're far from happy.

The book of Psalms deals a lot with these very human feelings. David didn't enjoy watching undeserving people prospering any more than we do. So, he talked it over with God. It's OK to do that, you know. God reads our hearts anyway, so it's not like we're telling him anything he doesn't already know. He's well aware when we think something is unfair. We can't fake our feelings with him. He knows when we're not happy. He knows when we don't understand the trial we may be going through. If we can be real with anyone, we can be real with God.

David found comfort in sharing these innermost feelings with God. It helped him work through some of his frustration and it also reminded him where he needed to be placing his focus. The good fortune of his enemies wasn't going to ruin David's day. He was going to keep his mind on God, obey his commandments, and trust that someday it would all even out. After all, true promotion, the kind that lasts through eternity, comes from God, and David knew that it was just a matter of time before his enemies would be seeing that for themselves.

Thoughts to Ponder

Is there someone in your life who has received a promotion that you feel he or she didn't deserve?

Do you think this person's promotion is the eternal kind, or is it something that will pass?

Bumper Sticker for the Day

Life's not fair—but God always is.

Scripture to Stand On

For I envied the arrogant when I saw the prosperity of the wicked.

PSALM 73:3

Hello Again, Lord ...

Lord, you are a fair and just God, and I know you will even the score if I just do my part and stay in the game.

43. Anonymous

I recently read in *People* magazine that Gilmore and Golda Reynolds—an unassuming, well-liked couple who lived modestly in Osgood, Indiana—died, leaving the town some $23 million. No one in the town, which boasts a population of only 1,852, knew of their vast wealth. The couple had managed to keep it, and much of their personal lives, private.

The people of Osgood aren't quite sure what they're going to do with all of that money, but they're excited about the possibilities. Already there's talk of an expanded library, new sidewalks, and a new YMCA. The money will be distributed in grants of one million dollars each year for the next several decades.

I found this story intriguing on many levels. Primarily, how could a couple amass that much wealth without anyone finding out about it? They lived well below their means (their home was listed on the market for only $65,000). They didn't flaunt the fact that they had made a fortune in the stock market. They treated everyone the same, and preferred to exhibit their generosity in a quiet, behind-the-scenes manner. They were also totally committed to each other. They must have gotten a kick out of knowing they were going to leave that kind of a gift to the town. It was their little secret.

This is the kind of generosity that God wants us all to have—the kind that will have us giving to others without expecting a single thing in return. The Reynoldses did their gift-giving anonymously. When you give anonymously, there's no way that your pride can enter into the picture, because no one knows you did it.

Thoughts to Ponder

Can you think of a time when you did a "secret" good deed for someone else?

Think of a "secret" good deed that you can do this week for someone in your life.

Bumper Sticker for the Day

> **Anonymity—
> the most sincere form of gift wrapping.**

Scripture to Stand On

I will abundantly bless her provision; I will satisfy her poor with bread.

PSALM 132:15, NKJV

Hello Again, Lord ...

Lord, your Word says that money isn't everything. Forgive us for having to be reminded so often of that fact.

44. Atonement

Those who follow the Jewish faith celebrate what they call a "Day of Atonement." It's a day set aside to try to work on a relationship that may have soured over the years. It's a day to let bygones be bygones, a day to forgive. It might be a good idea for the Christian faith to have a day like this too.

Granted, we're all supposed to live in a state of forgiveness—God has forgiven us, so we should forgive one another, right? Yet we're all human. Sometimes we hang on to old grudges as though they're collectibles, increasing in value with each passing year. Grudges don't gain value over the years, though. They just gain weight. They become heavier and heavier to carry and can cause all sorts of other problems. A broken relationship is often the underlying cause of anger, stress, and sometimes even depression.

So, if you're still not talking to that ex–best friend who flirted with the guy that you liked at camp last year, or if your third cousin who hurt your feelings four-and-a-half years ago still has her name crossed out in your telephone book, why not set your own "day of atonement" and give her a call?

Forgiving someone doesn't mean that what they did to you didn't hurt. Jesus forgave his accusers while hanging from the cross. He didn't hang there and pretend not to be in pain. The fact that he was able to forgive them in the midst of that pain, though, is what brought glory to God. And that's what true forgiveness is really all about.

Thoughts to Ponder

Do you think it would be a good idea for people of all faiths to have a Day of Atonement? Why?

Is there a broken relationship in your life that needs repairing?

Bumper Sticker for the Day

Forgiveness—a gift you give yourself.

Scripture to Stand On

If You, Lord, should mark iniquities, O Lord, who could stand?

PSALM 130:3, NKJV

Hello Again, Lord ...

Lord, repair my broken relationships, reinforcing the areas that need reinforcing and cutting away those areas that need cutting away.

45. Silence Isn't Always Golden

It doesn't matter if you're the next Amy Grant, Carman, or Sandi Patty; if you only sing in the shower, who's going to know? Mr. Clean? If you haven't heard, he hasn't been signing that many recording artists lately.

Even if you're funnier than Jay Leno or Mark Lowry, if you keep all your punch lines in your head, you're denying all of us some good laughs.

If you can paint like Van Gogh, play tennis like Andre Agassi, or know more about computers than Bill Gates, it doesn't matter unless you let people know. If Beethoven had just scribbled his symphonies on a piece of paper and then thrown them away, we would never have been able to appreciate his talent. If Celine Dion had sung only in her car on her way to school or work, who would have ever asked her to step up to the microphone?

All of us have been gifted in some way. We may still be trying to find out what our gifts are, but they're there. They came with the package. Yet if we never use them, and never let anyone else know about them, they're not doing us—or anyone else—any good. So use your talent every chance you get. Who knows? You just might be the next legend in the making.

Thoughts to Ponder

How do you feel God has gifted you?

Even if you don't know how God can use your talents, do you think that he does?

Bumper Sticker for the Day

> Unused gifts gather dust, not admiration.

Scripture to Stand On

I will instruct you and teach you in the way you should go;
I will counsel you and watch over you.

PSALM 32:8

Hello Again, Lord ...

May I show my gratitude for the gifts you've given me by doing something with them.

46. Out of Control

One morning as I drove my three sons to school, a car crossing the intersection pulled in front of us without warning, causing me to slam on my brakes and swerve. I managed to miss it, but unfortunately, my car began sliding out of control, heading directly for another car stopped in the left turn lane of the cross street.

I could see the terrified look on the driver's face as my vehicle headed right at him. I imagine I had the same look on my face. There wasn't anything either one of us could do. It all seemed so surreal. My foot was pressing the brake pedal all the way to the floor, yet we were still sliding. It was just a matter of time before my kids and I would be joining him in his front seat.

Bracing ourselves for certain impact, we prayed. I think I even closed my eyes. It was at the very last second, when we were just inches away from the other car's front door. I didn't want to see the crash. Hearing it was going to be bad enough.

Instead of hearing the sound of crunching metal, however, I felt the car suddenly jerk to a stop. I waited for a crash, but there was none. There was just the odor of burning rubber.

Slowly, I opened my eyes. The other car was still there. We were right up against it, but without any crunching noise, there couldn't have been a collision, right?

When I got out of the car to investigate, I discovered that the front bumper of our car had somehow come to rest on the other car's front tire. There was no wrinkled metal or broken glass. The only evidence that there had been any kind of problem at all was the fact that since I had been pressing down so hard on the car horn, and turning the steering wheel at the same time, the middle part of it had popped out of place and was now hanging in my lap by its wires.

There are times when our lives can seem out of control like that. Something, whether it's our own doing or the thoughtlessness of others, sends us sliding right into harm's way, and there's only one thing we can do—pray. Even when it looks like we're sure to crash, God always comes through, often at the last minute, not only saving us from sure death or injury, but proving once again that even when we're out of control, he never is.

Thoughts to Ponder

Have you experienced a period in your life when you have felt things were totally out of control?

Why is it a good idea to let God have control of our lives?

Bumper Sticker for the Day

> Sometimes "out of control"
> is the best place to be.

Scripture to Stand On

He alone is my rock and my salvation; he is my fortress, I will not be shaken.

PSALM 62:6

Hello Again, Lord ...

Lord, thank you for being in control ... especially when I'm not.

47. But Did He Really Mean It?

God hates all sin, but Proverbs 6:16-19 says there are six things that God really hates. That's right, it says he hates them. He even throws in a seventh one and calls them all an abomination. That's pretty strong. So, what are these seven deadly sins?

1. Haughty eyes.
2. A lying tongue.
3. Hands that shed innocent blood.
4. A heart that devises wicked schemes.
5. Feet that are quick to rush into evil.
6. A false witness who pours out lies.
7. A person who stirs up dissension among brethren.

Whoa, now wait a minute. I know he said all that, but did he really mean it? Why would that last one be listed with the others? I believe it's because of the destruction it causes. God doesn't like troublemakers. If we're getting on the telephone and stirring up discord within his church, he's not only displeased with our actions, he says it's an *abomination* to him. If we're telling half-truths or making up lies about someone else, he doesn't just wish we'd quit. He *hates* what we're doing.

David felt the effects of many of these sins firsthand. He was falsely accused. He was pursued by hands that would shed innocent blood. He had to deal with people who spoke lies against him and hearts that devised wicked schemes. God sustained him throughout his ordeal, but he had to have been very displeased with those who were behind these sinful actions.

So the next time we reach for that telephone or type that

e-mail to share the latest bit of news we've heard about someone else, we might want to stop and read this passage from
Proverbs again. As harmless as these actions seem, they're sin,
and God couldn't have been any more clear in his disdain for
them.

Thoughts to Ponder

If you honestly examined your actions, how many of these seven
sins have you been guilty of?

Why do you think these seven sinful actions are so repulsive
to God?

Bumper Sticker for the Day

> **If you can't say something nice about someone,
> you're not trying hard enough.**

Scripture to Stand On

Whoever slanders his neighbor in secret, him will I put to
silence; whoever has haughty eyes and a proud heart, him will
I not endure.

PSALM 101:5

Hello Again, Lord ...

Lord, help me to see the seriousness of my actions, especially
when they hurt another of your children.

48. Taking a Stand

Have you ever gotten a leg cramp in the middle of the night? You know, those fun ones that bolt you out of bed and set your feet to dancing, whether you like it or not.

Leg cramps usually come with no warning. You could be lying there in bed, deep in a wonderful dream, and all of a sudden, they'll hit. Ignoring them, hoping they'll go away, only makes them worse.

The best cure for a leg cramp is to get up, no matter how difficult a notion that is, and put your foot down. It won't be easy at first. In fact, it'll feel like your leg is a tree trunk that's jamming its way up your torso, but eventually you will manage to do it. Then, and only then, will the pain begin to subside.

Some of life's pains can be like leg cramps. One minute everything can be going along fine, but the next minute a problem can hit that bolts us out of our comfort, gets us up on our feet, and throws us into a panic. These life cramps come with no warning, and their pain can cause us to tense up and forget what normalcy was like.

The best thing to do at times like that is to get up, no matter how difficult that may be, and put your foot firmly on God's Word. It may hurt at first, but the more quickly you do it and the more firmly you stand, the sooner you'll be able to relax again.

Thoughts to Ponder

Have you ever hesitated to take a stand when you knew you should?

What will you do differently the next time you need to take a stand?

Bumper Sticker for the Day

> **The Bible is our muscle relaxer for life.**

Scripture to Stand On

My feet stand on level ground; in the great assembly I will praise the Lord.

PSALM 26:12

Hello Again, Lord ...

Lord, help me to know that taking a stand always feels better after I've done it.

49. No Time to Lose

Yesterday, we spent the day at the home of an eighty-year-old friend of the family. My son and his wife had stopped by the man's house to pick him up for a birthday party, and had made the unfortunate discovery that he had passed away a few nights before, on New Year's Eve. He didn't make it to the new millennium.

All that day, while waiting for the mortuary to come and pick up the body, we sat around his table and remembered his life. He had never married, but everyone was his family. He wasn't rich, but was one of the most generous people you would ever want to meet. He was sick, but rarely complained.

You're young now, but you're setting a pattern for your life that will become who you are, who people will describe when they're remembering you. What do you think they'll say? Will they remember you as a giver or a taker? A person who was content, or a complainer who didn't appreciate a single blessing you'd been given?

I lay awake in bed last night, thinking about how short life really is. Eighty is too young to die, yet most of us won't even make it to that age. The person we want to be remembered for is the person we need to start being now.

Thoughts to Ponder

Why do you think it's important to start now to become the person you want to be?

How do you want people to remember you at the end of your life?

Bumper Sticker for the Day

> **Live like someone else will be writing your eulogy ... because someone else will be.**

Scripture to Stand On

My days are like the evening shadow; I wither away like grass.

PSALM 102:11

Hello Again, Lord ...

Lord, help me to live the kind of life that pays tribute to you.

50. Humble Pie

Most of the writers I know don't have a problem with pride. They battle insecurity instead. As writers, we put our lives down on paper. We're open to other people's criticism, scrutiny, and judgment. Actors get to play someone other than themselves. Singers usually sing other people's words. But writers? It's just the paper and us. We bare our souls, and too often bare too much. So, while the writing life can be very fulfilling, it can also be humbling—especially when it comes to autograph signings.

When my very first book came out, the owner of a local religious bookstore, Mrs. Russo, a wonderful woman, offered to give me an autograph party. It was very kind of her, so I agreed. After all, signing books is what authors do. Well, most of them anyway. Only a handful of people showed up for this book signing, and four of those were my husband and children. Another person who did show up, though, was a newspaper reporter, and the next morning's headlines read, "Author's Hand Gets Rest at Autograph Signing."

My first Christian Booksellers' Convention wasn't any better. My autograph session was scheduled for the same time that Carman, Jerry Falwell, and Kenneth Taylor were signing. I'm not saying how long my line was, but I was signing my autographs in calligraphy.

Things like that don't happen just to me, however. I remember reading a piece written by Jack Smith, noted columnist for the *Los Angeles Times*. He was sharing a story about going to a garage sale one day and finding a book of his that he had autographed to "My good friends ..." among the items being sold that day for mere change. He didn't let it get him down, though. He had a good laugh, then wrote a funny column about it.

Being embarrassed or humbled isn't anything to fear. Experiences like that give us something to laugh about and remind us that we're human. When we no longer have those moments, or we pretend we don't, that's when our pride can grow to dangerous proportions. So the next time no one's in my autograph line, I won't take it personally. I'll just figure God wants me to brush up on my calligraphy.

Thoughts to Ponder

Think of a humbling incident that happened to you recently.

What have you learned, or can you learn, from it?

Bumper Sticker for the Day

> **He who can't laugh at himself leaves the job to others.**

Scripture to Stand On

You hear, O Lord, the desire of the afflicted; you encourage them, and you listen to their cry.

PSALM 10:17

Hello Again, Lord ...

Lord, help me to remember that humble pie can sometimes be the best dessert of all.

51. Change Your Mind

D o you ever find yourself thinking about things you shouldn't really be thinking about? I'm not talking about impure thoughts, although we need to guard our minds against those, too. What I'm referring to is negative thoughts.

If we're not careful, it's easy to let our minds tell us all the things we can't do, remind us of our failures, and convince us that God will never be able to use us because of them. Our minds can deceive us into thinking a situation is hopeless when, with God, a situation never is. Our mind can play a lot of tricks on us.

But do you know that you have the power to change your mind? If you find your mind telling you things that aren't true, or painting a picture much gloomier than reality, you can change your mind by feeding it new information. The next time your mind tells you you're a failure, remind it of a few of your successes. When your mind tells you that in spite of all your faith, a situation is hopeless, tell it that hopelessness isn't the absence of hope, it's the surrender of it, and you don't feel like surrendering just yet.

Your thoughts are under your control. If you don't want them to be negative, you have the power to change your mind. And in doing so, you just might change your situation, too, for the better.

Thoughts to Ponder

Throughout your day, would you say you think more positive thoughts or more negative thoughts?

Why do you think God wants us to keep our minds on positive things?

Bumper Sticker for the Day

> **Optimist:**
> Someone who doesn't need to see the sun
> to know it's still there behind the clouds.

Scripture to Stand On

It is good to praise the Lord and make music to your name, O Most High.

PSALM 92:1

Hello Again, Lord ...

Lord, help me to remember that my thoughts can either drain me or sustain me.

52. Nothing but the Truth

Have you ever been around someone who feels compelled to always tell "the truth," or at least his or her version of it, no matter who it hurts? "Do I like your new haircut? I hate it! Sorry, but that's just the way I feel."

"Your new boyfriend? Can we say 'loser'? I'm just calling it as I see it."

"I used to have a dress like yours, but I gave it away when it went out of style four years ago."

Someone once said that you should always tell the truth, but you don't always have to be telling the truth. That's a good way to put it. If your best friend's hair looks terrible, find something else about which to compliment her. If your brother's saxophone solo sounds like a cat caught in a fan belt, tell him how good he is at sports. Don't be like those who use truth as a license to hurt. There are all sorts of truths to choose from in any situation, at any given moment. Instead of selecting a truth that puts someone down, find a truth that lifts the person up and say that instead. Truth is a positive force. It should be used for good.

Thoughts to Ponder

When you feel compelled to tell "the truth" to someone, is it usually a truth that is positive or a truth that is negative?

How does it make you feel when someone points out an unkind "truth" to you?

Bumper Sticker for the Day

Honesty is the best policy ...
but sometimes silence can be just as good.

Scripture to Stand On

His speech is smooth as butter, yet war is in his heart; his words are more soothing than oil, yet they are drawn swords.

PSALM 55:21

Hello Again, Lord ...

Lord, help me to know that an honest tongue doesn't have to be a hurtful one.

53. What'd I Do?

The book of Psalms talks an awful lot about enemies. Enemies are like chicken pox. They're no fun to have, you might not have done anything to get them, and even when you do your best to deal with them, they can still leave scars. Often, enemies are born out of jealousy. Someone may not like you because you're better looking, you're more talented, you're more popular, you get better grades, or you dress better than they do. It doesn't make much sense to us now, and it didn't make sense to David either.

Saul was jealous of David. He was afraid that David was going to take over his throne. And so, Saul and his army tried to kill David, even though David had done nothing wrong. In fact, David had already been ordained of God, so Saul's pursuit was a futile effort anyway.

Still, David had to deal with Saul—an enemy he didn't ask for or deserve, but nonetheless had. So how did he do it? By leaving the matter to God. David shows us that we can sing when we're being unfairly persecuted, when we feel like we don't have a friend in the world. David kept a song in his heart and was eventually made king. Saul? He was killed in battle, and will always be remembered for his jealousy instead of his royalty.

Thoughts to Ponder

Do you have someone in your life who would like to see you fail?

Would you say this person's problem is with you or a battle within him- or herself?

Bumper Sticker for the Day

Love your enemies—it really irritates them.

Scripture to Stand On

May all who seek to take my life be put to shame and confusion; may all who desire my ruin be turned back in disgrace.

PSALM 40:14

Hello Again, Lord ...

Lord, even you had enemies. Help me to follow your example in dealing with mine.

54. Exits

One of my funniest childhood memories happened while playing mad scientist in the backyard with my sister. As we mixed and stirred our "secret potion," our dog lay nearby, napping in the sun. We continued to add ingredients until it became apparent that something special was needed. What could it be? Ah, yes ...

"We need the brain of a dog," one of us said menacingly. We were only joking, of course, and to my knowledge our dog couldn't speak English (unless he was taking night classes on the side), but as soon as he heard those words, he bolted up and took off, easily clearing our five-foot fence. We got a good laugh out of it, and to this day I don't know why he made his exit at that precise moment.

Human exits aren't usually that perfectly timed. We tend to remain in bad situations far too long, convinced that "things will get better." We stay long after our conscience has left because "it surely can't be as bad as it looks." Never mind that our instincts are telling us we should have gotten up and cleared that fence weeks, months, maybe even years before. For whatever reason, we can't seem to make our exit.

If we're hanging out with people we shouldn't be with or becoming involved in things we have no business being involved in, it's time to leave. Simple as that. And the good news is that every exit is also an entrance: an entrance to something else, often much better than we can imagine.

Thoughts to Ponder

Have you ever stayed in a situation long after you should have made your exit?

What are some good signs that it's time to make an exit?

Bumper Sticker for the Day

We can learn a lot from a tree ...
especially when to dig in our roots
and when to leave.

Scripture to Stand On

I said, "Oh, that I had the wings of a dove! I would fly away and be at rest."

PSALM 55:6

Hello Again, Lord ...

Lord, help me to know when it's time to make an exit from unhealthy situations, and give me the courage to do it.

55. No Room for Error

If the gospel is about anything, it's about grace. It's about forgiveness after we've made and admitted our mistakes. It's about second chances when we've totally messed up our first one. It's about getting up after we've fallen down again. And again. And again.

Even though there are spiritual second chances, however, there may be some situations where we won't get any physical ones. If we disobey our parents and go hang gliding in a thunderstorm after they've told us we can't, God can forgive our disobedience. But hours later, when we're still up there dodging lightning and floating around uncontrollably, saying "I'm sorry" might not be enough.

If we run away from home in the middle of a blizzard, God can forgive us. Our parents can forgive us, too. But if we become a live ice sculpture, frostbite could set in and we could lose parts of our bodies. We'll be forgiven, but we'll look a lot different without a nose.

There's a reason we're to obey. It's not to take away our freedom or to keep us from doing something we think we have to do. It's usually to protect us from something that could harm us. Yes, there will be times when we make the wrong choices, when we take a different route than we should. In those cases, it's important to note that God is always ready, willing, and able to forgive a repentant heart. But know, too, that you're running the risk that the price you pay for your disobedience may be more than you bargained for.

Thoughts to Ponder

Have you ever had to pay a higher price than you counted on for disobedience?

What would you do next time when confronted with a similar temptation?

Bumper Sticker for the Day

> **The best gift we can give ourselves
> is no regrets.**

Scripture to Stand On

Direct my footsteps according to your word; let no sin rule over me.

PSALM 119:133

Hello Again, Lord ...

Lord, thank you for second chances, but help me not to waste my first one.

56. Awards Night

What if people who gave acceptance speeches for awards or honors listed those people in their life whom they couldn't thank for their support instead of those who did encourage them? It would sound something like this:

"I really can't thank my friend Marion, who has never said an encouraging word to me in all the years I've known her. She's been there beside me every step of the way with her cutting remarks, her 'Why don't you just give it up?' advice, and her all too obvious jealousies. I'd also like not to thank my mother, who has criticized every move I have ever made and has always told me that I wouldn't amount to anything. Last and certainly least, I'd like not to thank my sister, Sarah, who tried her best to sabotage every good thing that ever happened in my life."

People who receive awards, though, don't list their discouragers. It would sound tacky, and besides, why waste stage time on people who don't deserve it? They'd much rather list those real friends and loving family members who have been there for them through thick and thin, who have always believed in them, and who have never said a discouraging word.

Think about it. If your friends at church or school, members of your family, or even acquaintances were to receive an award, would you be named among their encouragers and given a glowing tribute, or would your name make their "critical list"?

Thoughts to Ponder

Think it over—do you think you're more of an encourager or a discourager?

In the spiritual world, whose job is it to be an encourager? Whose job is it to be a discourager? Which side are you helping by your actions?

Bumper Sticker for the Day

> **Bring out the best in those around you and you'll be surrounded by the best.**

Scripture to Stand On

Scorn has broken my heart and has left me helpless; I looked for sympathy, but there was none, for comforters, but I found none.

PSALM 69:20

Hello Again, Lord ...

Lord, don't let me be stingy with your gift of encouragement.

57. The Great Pretender

Over the last twenty years, I've worked with many actors, in both church drama and television. I've seen a lot of performances. Some of those performances have been amateur, most have been good, and a few have even been brilliant. The best performances, of course, are the ones that are so convincing the audience can't tell where the performer's personality ends and the character's personality begins.

Not all the acting you'll come across in life happens on stage, though. Sometimes it's just ordinary people playing a role, pretending to be someone other than who they really are. They say and seemingly do all the right things, but upon closer inspection, you find it's all been an act. There are hidden motives behind every kind gesture they do, and their calculated actions are nothing more than posturing.

God doesn't want us acting out the role of Christian. There won't be a heavenly version of the Oscar for the best Christlike performance delivered on earth. He wants real people living out real faith to the best of their ability. He wants people who might stumble over their lines from time to time, maybe even miss a cue or two, but who aren't reading from a script. Just living out their faith, ad-libbing as they go, sincerely from their hearts.

Thoughts to Ponder

Have you ever caught yourself "acting" out your Christianity?

Why do you think God prefers us to just be real?

Bumper Sticker for the Day

Faked faith fails.

Scripture to Stand On

O Lord, you have searched me and you know me. You know when I sit and when I rise; you perceive my thoughts from afar.

PSALM 139:1-2

Hello Again, Lord ...

Lord, when it comes to my faith, may it never be an act.

58. Crossing the Line

One of the hardest lessons young comedians have to learn is where the "line" is. The "line" I'm referring to is that invisible line a comedian crosses over when he or she goes from funny to offensive. Comedians run the risk of crossing over that line every time they perform.

The main problem is the fact that the line is not definitive. It can be in one place for one comedian, but in an entirely different place for another. Why? Most of it has to do with trust. This is especially true for comedians who perform in churches. If the comedian has already earned a reputation for loving God, respecting the church, and abiding by the principles of faith, then he or she can probably get away with a little more poking fun at church life. If, however, the comedian hasn't earned that trust, then jokes about the church are going to be suspect. Instead of laughing *about* church life, the audience figures the comic is laughing *at* church life.

There's a line you don't want to cross in joking with your friends, too. If you haven't earned enough trust that your friends know your teasing is genuinely good-natured and coming from a friendly place, then you probably shouldn't risk it. Often friends won't tell you when you've inadvertently crossed that line and hurt their feelings. They'll just keep taking your teasing with a disguised laugh until one day they don't feel like laughing anymore. Or hanging around with you.

So the next time you feel like teasing one of your friends, ask yourself whether that friend has enough trust in your friendship to see the humor and laugh with you. Otherwise you just might be laughing alone.

Thoughts to Ponder

Do you think you've ever inadvertently hurt one of your friends by your teasing?

Why do you think you need to be sensitive to the feelings of others when you're joking with them?

Bumper Sticker for the Day

> **If you must take an offensive position, be sure you're on the football field.**

Scripture to Stand On

Let the words of my mouth and the meditation of my heart be acceptable in Your sight, O Lord, my strength and my redeemer.

PSALM 19:14, NKJV

Hello Again, Lord ...

Lord, help me to remember that when it comes to teasing, there's often more hurt than humor.

59. Sorry, Not a Winner

There it was, written right on the candy wrapper. "Winner." I couldn't believe it! I didn't know what I had won, but I had won something. The wrapper said I had. It said I was a winner. Who's going to argue with a candy wrapper?

After I finished chewing the last bite of the candy—first things first, of course—I decided I should check the wrapper to see what it was I had won. Maybe it was a new car. Or a new computer. Or maybe even a thousand dollars. Or a hundred dollars. Why, I'd have been happy to win twenty bucks.

The wrapper had been torn, so I had to put the pieces of the puzzle back together before I'd know what I could celebrate. Too bad. Because once the pieces were reunited, I could see that while my side of the wrapper said "Winner," the other side said, "Sorry, Not a." While I was assuming I had won something, I had won nothing. With all the pieces of the message in place, it was plain to see that all I had to show for my efforts was the short-lived taste of a candy bar.

Some of the temptations we face in life can make us think we're winners, too, at least from our angle. We see the word "Winner" and rush blindly to claim our prize, but we're reading only half the wrapper. Once we get a good look at all the pieces, we find that we haven't really won anything. The temptation actually said, "Sorry, Not a Winner," and all we're left with is the short-lived taste of something we really didn't need in the first place, and that's nothing to celebrate.

Thoughts to Ponder

Have you ever thought you had "won" something, only to discover it was no prize?

Why is it important to remember that even when we lose, God can still make us winners?

Bumper Sticker for the Day

> **Some prizes aren't worth winning.**

Scripture to Stand On

But you, O Lord, are a compassionate and gracious God, slow to anger, abounding in love and faithfulness.

PSALM 86:15

Hello Again, Lord ...

Lord, help me to keep my eyes focused on the finish line, the most important part of the race.

60. High Flying

I've traveled in a variety of airplanes during my life. My least favorite planes are the older ones—you know, the ones where the in-flight entertainment is Orville and Wilbur Wright's home movies. Maybe it's just me, but I prefer airplanes that have been built within the last three decades.

I had the misfortune of flying on an older plane recently. I tried not to worry about it, but it wasn't very comforting to hear the stewardess refer to the area over the engines as "the smoking section." I do have to hand it to the mechanics, though. That was some of the most creative use of duct tape I've ever seen.

Needless to say, it wasn't a very smooth flight. Going through unstable air in an unstable airplane makes for some terrifying moments. We made it, but I don't think I'd want to repeat the experience.

Going through an unstable life depending on an unstable faith can have some terrifying moments, too. We often overlook the importance of maintaining our faith, permitting it to continually deteriorate. After years of neglect, we wonder why it's rusted and cracking and leaving us stranded. We figure it's easier to duct tape over our emotional injuries than to replace bad attitudes with new and improved ones. We limp along, trying our best to stay in the air. But without a dependable faith, it's just a matter of time before we hit some turbulence, start spiraling downward, and maybe even crash.

Thoughts to Ponder

What are you doing to keep your faith in good condition?

Why do you think it's important to maintain a strong faith?

Bumper Sticker for the Day

> **Faith is powered by prayer.**
> **Recharge it daily.**

Scripture to Stand On

From the ends of the earth I call to you, I call as my heart grows faint; lead me to the rock that is higher than I.

PSALM 61:2

Hello Again, Lord ...

Lord, remind me to give my faith routine maintenance checks.

61. Next Question, Please

In school, I was never one to raise my hand and ask a question. I don't know why I didn't want to ask questions. Maybe it's because I tend to be shy. Maybe I thought they were dumb questions. Maybe it was before lunch and I didn't have the energy to lift my arm. Who knows? The bottom line, though, is that I missed plenty of opportunities to learn just because of my hesitation to ask.

If it hasn't already happened, chances are you're going to go through a period of questioning about life. You're going to wonder why you're here. You'll ask yourself if God really does exist or if he's just a figment of a lot of people's imaginations. You'll wonder what this life we're living is all about. You'll have questions. Ask them.

There's nothing wrong with asking questions. Our inquisitiveness doesn't bother God. He created us. He gave us that desire to question. He knows that we want answers, and he's ready and willing to give them. He might not always give us the answers we want to hear. He might not answer our questions as quickly as we want them answered, either. But he will answer.

Questions? We have plenty of them. Answers? God's got them all.

Thoughts to Ponder

Is there a question that you've been wanting to ask God? What is it?

Why do you think God wants us to share our doubts with him?

Bumper Sticker for the Day

> **Got doubts? God can handle them.**

Scripture to Stand On

Trust in him at all times, O people; pour out your hearts to him, for God is our refuge.

PSALM 62:8

Hello Again, Lord ...

Lord, help me to trust you as much with the things I don't understand as I do with the things that I do understand.

62. Assumptions

This year I developed a minor foot problem that required corrective shoes and a pair of orthotics. Orthotics are special inserts that compensate for whatever imperfections your feet may have. Many professional athletes wear them, and I had thought they were the greatest thing to come along since e-mail. Until the other day.

I had just parked my car and was walking into Kinko's. Now, the Kinko's near my home is located next to a very quaint muffin restaurant with floor-to-ceiling windows. It's usually packed. The food is great there, so it's no wonder.

I got out of my car, basking in the fact that I had scored the number-one parking space, and began the thirty-foot or so walk to Kinko's. After about three steps, my left foot somehow slid off my orthotic, twisting my ankle. My arms automatically flew up in the air to balance me, then I stumbled five or six more feet before coming to a stop ... in a pothole, where I promptly tripped again, stumbling a few more steps before tripping on my now loosened shoelace. All of this was within clear view of everyone in the restaurant.

I was sure they assumed that I was either: (a) drunk (I've never had an alcoholic beverage in my life); (b) mentally unbalanced (I've worked with Mark Lowry for over fifteen years, but I don't think there's been any permanent damage); or (c) trying out for the slapstick version of the Nutcracker Suite.

I don't know, but I would venture to say that most people would probably guess "a" or "b." That's because we tend to judge people from our point of view. But our point of view doesn't always include all the facts. All those people saw was a lady staggering through the parking lot and flailing her arms.

They didn't know about the orthotic, the pothole, or the loose shoelaces.

I had a good laugh at myself over the ordeal. I'm sure it looked pretty funny to the onlookers, too. But it reminded me of an important fact of life. No matter what we see or hear, we should never jump to conclusions about somebody until we're sure we've got the whole picture.

Thoughts to Ponder

Have you ever jumped to conclusions about a situation without first checking out the facts?

Has anyone ever misjudged you about something? How did it make you feel?

Bumper Sticker for the Day

Gossip:
the fastest way for misinformation to travel.

Scripture to Stand On

But God is the Judge: He puts down one, and exalts another.

PSALM 75:7, NKJV

Hello Again, Lord ...

Lord, remind me that assumptions are like library books. You should check them out before taking them home with you.

63. That Stinging Feeling

Have you ever had to stand by and watch your pride take a beating? It doesn't feel good, does it? In fact, it hurts. Sometimes a lot. We don't like to be cut down to size, especially when we're feeling smaller than life already. We don't enjoy spending hours convincing ourselves how much we really do deserve a certain recognition, promotion, or position, only to find out later that not many other people agree. It takes a lot of energy to hype ourselves up with positive input like "I really AM the best!" or "I'm just who they need for the job!" only to find out later that it was someone else they needed. We weren't even a close second. Our pride, however short-lived, can't help but start to sting a little.

Even though it stings, it's healthy to have our pride cut down to size every so often. If that didn't happen, it would become so overgrown that no one would ever be able to stand being around us. If we're smart, we'll take the experience and learn from it. If we're not, we'll rebel. "How can they treat me this way?" "I deserve more than this!" "Don't they know who I am?!" That kind of attitude may help our ego feel better for the moment, but it'll hurt us in the long run. Pride takes up room in your heart that God wants to occupy.

Thoughts to Ponder

Has your pride ever taken a beating?

Has any good come from it?

Bumper Sticker for the Day

> **We have plenty of things to be proud of,
> but a prideful spirit isn't one of them.**

Scripture to Stand On

The Lord preserves the faithful, but the proud he pays back in full.

PSALM 31:23

Hello Again, Lord ...

Lord, thank you for the times I've been humbled and for the good that has come from them.

64. Rescued

It was the lead story on all the news channels that evening. A young boy had been playing near the rain-swollen Los Angeles River and had been swept away by the raging current. One of the members of the search-and-rescue team had positioned himself on a tree branch that extended over the water, a mile or so ahead of his path. If the boy could maneuver his way near the branch, the rescue worker would then be able to grab him and lift him out of the water. It required precise timing. It also required superhuman strength from the rescue worker. But the plan worked and the boy was saved. The entire city breathed a collective sigh of relief.

There will be times in our lives when we're called upon to have superhuman strength. There will be people who cross our path who will need us to reach out to them and not let go, no matter what. They'll be trapped in a current that's taking them nowhere but down. Of course, just as the boy had to maneuver his way to the rescue worker, these people have to want to help themselves. Once they've reached out for help, however feeble that reach might be, it'll be up to us to decide whether we're going to extend a hand to them, or let them float on by, ultimately to drown.

Thoughts to Ponder

Is there someone you know who could use a hand to help lift him or her out of a difficult situation?

In what ways can you reach out your hand to this person?

Bumper Sticker for the Day

It doesn't matter how good the help is
if it comes too late.

Scripture to Stand On

Show the wonder of your great love, you who save by your right hand those who take refuge in you from their foes.

PSALM 17:7

Hello Again, Lord ...

Lord, help me to be aware of those around me who need a helping hand to safety.

65. The Family Exchange

We've all been given gifts that we couldn't wait to take back to the store. That outfit your Aunt Paula bought for you last Christmas, the one with the zebra stripes and rhinestones. That belt buckle your grandfather bought you, the one that's so big it throws out your back every time you wear it. That CD of the "Top Ten Polka Hits of All Time" that your Uncle Ned bought you. As soon as you opened them, you knew you would soon be standing in the returns line, trying to exchange them for something else.

Have you ever wished you could exchange certain members of your family in the same way? Maybe you'd like to exchange your sister for one who wouldn't pick on you so much. Or you may want to trade your brother in for one who wouldn't spend so much time with his friends and so little time with you. Perhaps your parents are the ones you'd like to exchange. Maybe you'd rather have a mom and dad who didn't fight so much. Or gave you more freedom.

No matter how much we may wish there were an exchange line for family members, there isn't. Unless our safety is endangered, we usually have to stay with the family we've been given. But that doesn't mean we can't do our part to make things better. Your family may not know how much their actions are hurting you. Say something. Give them a chance to change. Often, people don't realize how their behavior is affecting those around them until it's pointed out to them. Things might not change. But then again, they might.

Communication is the key to any healthy relationship. Granted, there are a few family members we just have to love in spite of their bad behaviors. Every family has one or two. Other difficult family members, though, might actually appreciate our honesty and alter their actions enough to get us out of that exchange line and make us truly appreciate the family God has given us.

Thoughts to Ponder

Is there someone in your family with whom you're having difficulty getting along?

What changes are you praying for God to make in that person? What changes are you praying for God to make in yourself?

Bumper Sticker for the Day

> **Don't feel so bad.**
> **Even the first family was dysfunctional.**

Scripture to Stand On

I will extol the Lord at all times; his praise will always be on my lips.

PSALM 34:1

Hello Again, Lord ...

Lord, thank you for earthly families and the love they provide us, and thank you for filling in the gap when they don't.

66. Dirty Hands

When I was little, I used to love to make mud pies. No one ever ate them—foreshadowing my future culinary talents—but that didn't matter. I was having a good time just dipping my hands into the muddy mess and scooping a pile of it into each pie tin. That's the only way to make a mud pie. You've got to get dirty.

Sometimes to accomplish what we're meant to accomplish in life, we've got to be willing to get our hands dirty, too. By "dirty" I don't mean doing things that God wouldn't approve of. I'm talking about good, hard work.

If you spend the summer helping missionaries in a foreign country build a new church, you're going to get dirty. If you help serve meals to the homeless or to shut-ins, you're going to get dirty. If you volunteer to work in the church nursery or children's church, you're going to get dirty. If you try to help someone who's on a path to destruction, you're going to get dirty. Much of God's work involves getting dirty. He doesn't need workers who wear spiritual surgical gear, afraid to get close enough to make any real difference in anyone's life. He needs people who'll jump in, see what needs to be done, and get the job completed.

So don't be afraid to get your hands dirty for God. Dirt easily washes away, but the fruit of your labor won't.

Thoughts to Ponder

When's the last time you got your hands dirty for God?

Why do you think God wants us to be willing to get dirty for him?

Bumper Sticker for the Day

> **God—the world's first
> equal opportunity employer.**

Scripture to Stand On

Those who sow in tears will reap with songs of joy.

PSALM 126:5

Hello Again, Lord ...

Lord, when it comes to your work, may I see the value of the harvest before I weigh the cost of the labor.

67. Knee Bowling

Recently, I went bowling with my sister, Melva, and my niece, Lisa. I hadn't been bowling in years, but I do enjoy the sport and used to be fairly good at it. (I'd only roll the ball down the wrong alley once or twice per game.) So, naturally, I was looking forward to impressing everyone with my well-honed skill and natural grace with a bowling ball.

Lisa must have sensed my anticipation and excitement, because she listed me first on the score sheet. Confident, I arose from my seat, picked up the ball, and struck my usual bowling pose. Once properly positioned, I took my aim, then began walking toward the pins. One ... two ... three steps. Now, mere inches from the foul line, I leaned over, crouching my body with my left leg elevated ever so slightly into the air. But instead of releasing the ball in one fluid motion, I somehow crossed the foul line, triggering a loud buzzer.

Startled, my right leg leaped up to join my left, and the next thing I knew, I had landed squarely on both knees, and the ball had landed safely in the gutter. After that, it was hard to convince anyone that I had any real talent as a bowler. Whatever trophies I have on my mantel can never erase the image of me airborne that night on Lane 18.

Do you know that some of us display "trophies" as proof of our walk with the Lord? Such a person might point to their work in children's church or convalescent homes as "proof" of faith. But the minute there's a test of the heart, an opportunity to display a truly Christlike attitude—unselfish, kind, patient, longsuffering—we fail the test. We've got the pose right, but instead of throwing a strike, we fall flat on our knees.

Maybe that's where God wants us. After all, it doesn't matter how many "trophies" we have on our mantel heralding our good works; what matters is what God sees in us, and how we act at those times when it really counts.

Thoughts to Ponder

When you evaluate your walk with the Lord, which do you weigh more heavily—your works or your attitude?

Why do you think being a Christian is more about heart than about performance?

Bumper Sticker for the Day

> **When you fall, the best place to land
> is on your knees.**

Scripture to Stand On

Their hearts were not loyal to him, they were not faithful to his covenant.

PSALM 78:37

Hello Again, Lord ...

Lord, thank you for allowing the bruises that have helped me learn to walk.

68. Is Anybody There?

Do you ever feel like your prayers aren't reaching God? You say them, but it's as though St. Peter intercepts them at the gate and just takes a memo. So there you sit, with your prayer in an "incoming" box somewhere in heaven, waiting for God to get around to reading it, much less answering it. Or so you think.

Waiting for God to answer a prayer, or to acknowledge it in some way, is one of the toughest kinds of waiting there is. It's even worse than standing in line at the Department of Motor Vehicles. (It's easy to feel like they don't hear you there either.) We want our prayers answered right now. We don't want to have to wait. God has already promised to answer them, so why is he making us wait so long? Why does it seem like he's not even there?

Prayer requires trust. We have to trust that God hears us the second we pray. No one's taking any memos, and God doesn't keep business hours. He's there 24-7, whether we see anything happening or not. Often we don't. But we still have to believe that God is busy working behind the scenes on our behalf. When the time's right, our answer will come, and then we'll know beyond any doubt that God really has been listening all along.

Thoughts to Ponder

What need are you praying for right now that God doesn't seem to be answering?

Why do you think you might have to wait for your answer?

Bumper Sticker for the Day

> **When you pray to God,
> you'll never get an answering machine.**

Scripture to Stand On

Do not withhold your mercy from me, O Lord; may your love and your truth always protect me.

PSALM 40:11

Hello Again, Lord ...

Lord, thank you for always being there ... even when it may seem like you're not.

69. Behind You All the Way

I once went on a bike ride with a leadership group at my school. It was about a five-mile ride to a nearby park, where we were going to have a picnic and play a few games before returning home. Since the trek never seemed to take that long in a car, I agreed to go along. How bad could it be?

It wasn't long before I found out. All the other girls had three-speed and ten-speed bicycles. My bike had only one speed. And most of the path was uphill. That's not my favorite direction.

I didn't give up, though. I pedaled behind the rest of the group as best I could, maintaining no more than a two-block distance between us. They were always in sight, but I wouldn't have been of any immediate help to any of them, nor they to me, had an emergency risen.

Have you ever encountered a problem in life, only to discover your friends are about two blocks ahead of you? They're still within sight, so you know they haven't totally abandoned you, but they're not close enough to be of any help, either. "You need a ride to the game tonight? Gee, I sure wish I could help, but I'm doing my best to just keep up my own pace," they whine. Or, "You need to talk? Not right now. Can't you see I've got my own problems?"

Maybe you've been that kind of friend to others. You'd love to be there for them, but you have so much on your own calendar, there's no way you can fit another thing in.

Friends. Sometimes all we see of each other is our backs.

Thoughts to Ponder

Would you say you're a friend who can be counted on?

Which of your friends have always been there for you? Think about this before you answer because the answer may surprise you.

Bumper Sticker for the Day

> **One true friend is better than a roomful of superficial ones.**

Scripture to Stand On

Look to my right and see; no one is concerned for me.... I cry to you, O Lord; I say "You are my refuge, my portion in the land of the living."

PSALM 142:4-5

Hello Again, Lord ...

When my friends need me, may they not have to look too hard to find me.

70. It Doesn't Compute

When it comes to computers, you need to follow the manufacturer's rules of operation. I found that out the hard way. Last night, I shut down my computer without closing what I needed to close first, and now I'm paying the price for my thoughtless error. I've lost my modem, my internet server, my sound card, my mind, and who knows what else. Well, I haven't actually lost them. My computer just doesn't know where they are. Now I can't finish my work, get my e-mail, go on-line, or hear those cute little beeper noises every time I turn on my computer. All because I didn't follow the manufacturer's instructions.

God gave us his rules of operation for life. They can be found in the Bible, and they're called the Ten Commandments. Or the Two Commandments, if you prefer Jesus' version: "Love the Lord thy God with all thy heart, soul, and strength. And love thy neighbor as thyself." If you follow these two commandments, the others will fall into place.

But whether it's the Ten Commandments or the Two Commandments, why do you think God wanted us to have these rules? Probably so we wouldn't shut down like my computer did (figuratively speaking, of course). God knows there's a high price to pay for some of our thoughtless errors. If you shoplift, you could go to jail. If you disrespect your mother and father, they could ground you until your wedding day. If you bear false witness against someone, you could ruin that person's reputation and your credibility.

If you follow God's rules, though, you'll always be fully operational.

Thoughts to Ponder

Why do you think God gave us rules to follow?

What do you think society would be like without God's rules of order?

Bumper Sticker for the Day

> **The Ten Commandments—
> our operating instructions for life.**

Scripture to Stand On

I have not departed from your laws, for you yourself have taught me.

PSALM 119:102

Hello Again, Lord ...

Lord, thank you for your rules, for they bring order to my life.

71. Unearned Love

Do you know what it's like to be loved unconditionally? No matter what you do or don't do, you're confident that love will never be taken away. Perhaps your parents love you unconditionally. If not your parents, maybe it's one of your grandparents. Maybe it's an uncle or an aunt or a friend who loves you without your having to do a single thing to earn it. Or perhaps it's your pastor or youth leader. If you've ever been loved unconditionally, you know how awesome that kind of love is. It gives you a wonderful sense of self-worth because you know your value isn't tied to your accomplishments or mistakes. It comes from just being you.

Unfortunately, many of us know what the other kind of love feels like, too—love that we have to work for, and fear losing every time we mess up. "If I could just be good enough, maybe they'd love me," we think. Or, "I really failed this time. They'll probably never forgive me."

There's a big difference between unconditional love and conditional love. One makes you want to do good so that you won't be hurt by losing or never gaining that love in the first place. The other makes you want to do good because you already are loved, and you wouldn't want to hurt the person who believes in you so much.

God's love is the unconditional kind. You don't have to perform a long list of good deeds for him to love you. He's not going to withhold it if you do something wrong, either. Naturally, he doesn't want you to do wrong, and you show your love and respect for him by following his commandments. But his love isn't subject to our good or bad behavior. It wasn't when he sent his Son to die on the cross, and it isn't now.

So if you're trying to earn God's love, or if you're afraid of losing it should you trip up, forget it. It can't be done. You never earned it in the first place. It was a gift.

Thoughts to Ponder

Do you have someone in your life who loves you unconditionally?

Whom do you love unconditionally?

Bumper Sticker for the Day

> **He who had more cause than we to impose conditions on love, didn't.**

Scripture to Stand On

For you are great and do marvelous deeds; you alone are God.

PSALM 86:10

Hello Again, Lord ...

Lord, in a world that loves with conditions, thank you for not attaching any to yours.

72. 20-20 Life Vision

Recently, my son Tony, his fiancée Crystal, and I were at a bank in Van Nuys, California. Tony and I were standing at the ATM when we heard a gunshot. At first we thought a car had backfired, but then there followed three or four more shots. Tony quickly looked in the direction of the gunfire and saw a man perched behind a car with a gun in his hand. There was another man on the ground, with a circle of people standing off to the side watching. After six shots, Tony figured, the man was surely dead.

"Duck!" Tony yelled to me, motioning me to get behind the building. I did, but in the commotion dropped my bank card. There was a man in line behind us, and since I didn't want him to take advantage of the situation and make a withdrawal from my account, I yelled to Tony, "Get my card! Get my card!" (We think about strange things in a moment of panic.)

Tony picked up the card, then ran as fast as he could toward his car, where Crystal was sitting, apparently unaware of the imminent danger we were all in. There was another shot. "Get down, Tony!" I yelled. "Get down!" Tony ducked and continued toward the car. Meanwhile, the man who had been in line behind us just stood there watching us, rather than watching the gunfight. That seemed a little strange to me, but maybe he was in on it with them, I thought.

On the way to the car, Tony also noticed that no one else in the vicinity of the bank was reacting in any way. A man had just had multiple bullets fired into him not fifty feet from the bank, and everyone else was walking along calm as you please. A uniformed police officer was now even walking toward us, instead of walking toward the victim. Had the whole world seen so much violence, it just didn't faze people anymore?

Finally, the policeman said, "Sorry about that. They're filming a movie, *Final Payback.*" A movie! We lost two years of our lives for a *movie?* "But you guys were so good," he continued, "they should give you a part!" Actually, if they'd just get the ATM videotape, they'd have quite a good scene there. Our terror was convincing, I'm sure. Tony and I laughed the rest of the day about the incident. Looking back on it now that our hearts have stopped fibrillating, it really was pretty funny.

Sometimes we can react to a situation from the way our mind interprets it, instead of from reality. Three hours go by and no one's called us yet, so we tell ourselves that we have no friends. We don't have enough money to buy that new dress we want, so we grumble about being "poor," when the truth is we haven't missed a single meal yet. As you go through life, make sure you're seeing and reacting to reality, and not the scene fear or your own desires is painting for you.

Thoughts to Ponder
Have you ever grumbled about something that, in reality, wasn't as bad as you thought?

Why do you think it's important to react to reality, rather than to what fear or our own desire is telling us?

Bumper Sticker for the Day

> Reality—it's a nice place to visit,
> but some people just don't want to live there.

Scripture to Stand On

This is the day the Lord has made; let us rejoice and be glad in it.

PSALM 118:24

Hello Again, Lord ...

Lord, help me to remember that life's dramatic enough without adding my own drama to it.

73. Feeding the Needy

When Y2K fear was running rampant and being sold for a goodly price, many of us took to stocking up on food. If you didn't lose your head, you probably stocked up on enough for a long weekend without power. If you got caught up in the scare, you may have stored more. Lots of food. Barrels full. Closets full. Rooms full.

News organizations began to suggest that people could get rid of the surplus food by donating it to soup kitchens and other charities. It was the missions' lucky day. After all, we're talking about pounds and pounds of rice and beans, not just the little seven-ounce packages that usually get donated to shelters. And the meats? Forget those nasty little canned wienies. Most of us stocked up on good meats—canned roast beef, canned chicken, maybe even some caviar or liver paté.

Yes, homeless shelters had every right to be excited. No more outdated cans of garbanzo beans or discolored cans of beets. This year their clientele will be eating like royalty. That's because most of us found ways to be creative with our own stockpile. It was our survival food. Who could, or would want to, survive on just turnip greens and okra?

Then there's the water. We had gallons of it put away. The good stuff. Not just what we stored in our old milk cartons, but natural spring and Perrier. Some of us even invested in generators, in batteries, or spent thousands of dollars updating our computers, cars, and whatever else we thought we had to do. Could we afford it? Probably not, but we found a way. I suppose the point I'm making is this: it's amazing how much spare money we all found to feed the starving when we thought the starving were going to be us.

Thoughts to Ponder

Why do you think God wants us to care about the hungry?

How do you think God feels when we, who have never gone a full day without a meal, don't appreciate how blessed we are?

Bumper Sticker for the Day

> **Give good food to the food banks.**
> **You might have to eat it someday.**

Scripture to Stand On

But the needy will not always be forgotten, nor the hope of the afflicted ever perish.

PSALM 9:18

Hello Again, Lord ...

Lord, help me to be as generous to others as I am to myself.

74. Complications

Complications—we don't enjoy them when they come up in life, but without them things would get pretty boring. Imagine a football game where nothing happens. One team gets in position, the ball is hiked and passed. The opposing team simply simply watches as the ball is passed from player to player. Eventually, the ball makes it into the end zone and a touchdown is scored. That'd be fine for the first touchdown, but imagine the entire game being played that way, with no opposition or interference of any kind. It wouldn't be much of a game, would it? Even the sports announcers would be falling asleep.

Life has to have complications, too. That's what keeps it interesting. We don't like them. We'd much rather go along without any interference from anyone. We'd much rather score touchdown after touchdown by just running the length of the field or passing the ball to another teammate without having to deal with the opposing side. But it doesn't work that way. Life does have its share of fouls, interceptions, and tackles. God, though, has promised to help us with each complication as it arises. He's promised to be there through the whole game, helping us make the right plays and keeping us from getting tackled by more than we can bear.

Thoughts to Ponder

Do you have any complications that you're having to deal with right now?

When you win a game where there have been a lot of complications, is the victory sweeter?

Bumper Sticker for the Day

> **Life may be a roller coaster,**
> **but God's our safety bar.**

Scripture to Stand On

God is our refuge and strength, an ever present help in trouble.

PSALM 46:1

Hello Again, Lord ...

Thank you, Lord, for being the best coach for life anyone could ask for.

75. Keep Out!

I drove by a house once that had an eight-foot barbed wire fence erected around it. It was a regular tract home, so, needless to say, it caught my attention. There was a large, handmade sign stuck in the lawn that expressed the owner's feelings. It was hard to read as I drove by because it was hand-printed and there was a lot of text, but I did see the word "aliens" several times throughout, so I assumed he was either warning his space creatures to stay away or inviting them over for brunch.

Now, most of us don't lose sleep over the notion of aliens. They're good movie material, but beyond that, we're not putting them on our Christmas list. The fact that the home's owner believed in aliens isn't even the point I'm wanting to make. Regardless of why this person chose to erect his fence and become such a recluse, the bottom line is, he did it. He erected a physical fence to let others know of his emotional one.

Most people don't give us that much to go on. We can't see the emotional walls they've built around themselves. Their houses look just like ours—no barbed wire or handwritten signs screaming out for help. But the people are just as incarcerated by their own fears, and just as alone.

We can pass them day after day, commenting or even grumbling about the wall they've built, or we can walk up and knock on the door.

Thoughts to Ponder

What do you think makes some people build emotional fences?

Have you ever built an emotional fence around yourself?

Bumper Sticker for the Day

A fortress looks a lot more friendly
once someone finds the drawbridge.

Scripture to Stand On

God sets the lonely in families, he leads forth the prisoners
with singing.

PSALM 68:6

Hello Again, Lord ...

Lord, let me see the emotional fences that others have built, and
do my part to help bring them down.

76. I Could Use a Little Help

Do you sometimes feel like Martha in the Bible? You're the one doing all the work while your sister is just sitting at Jesus' feet, so to speak, acting oh so holy. You're mopping the kitchen floor while she's off reading her Bible somewhere. You're dusting the furniture while she's inviting neighborhood kids to your church's vacation Bible school. You're desperately trying to make the bed while she's praying at the foot of it.

Not that you begrudge her time with the Lord. As a matter of fact, you'd love to have some yourself. You'd love to just sit and pray and study God's Word, but then who'd clean the house? Someone has to dust and mop and make the beds. Surely, God wouldn't want you living in a toxic waste dump, right? If only your sister would help you with some of the chores, then you *both* could read, and pray, and grow closer to God. But nooooooo, she's too busy trying to make a good impression on the Master.

In the Bible, Martha's hard work didn't go unnoticed by Jesus. He appreciated what she was doing, but he also knew how little time he had left on the earth. The house could be cleaned later. Jesus wanted to spend time with his friends, not watch Martha clean the house. He knew they could work for him, but on this day, he just wanted to enjoy their company.

Thoughts to Ponder

With whom do you identify more—Mary or Martha?

Do you think Jesus wants to spend more time with you?

Bumper Sticker for the Day

**Are you so busy working for God
that you've forgotten to check in with him?**

Scripture to Stand On

Every day I will praise you and extol your name for ever and
ever.

PSALM 145:2

Hello Again, Lord ...

Lord, maybe the reason I'm running out of time in my day is
because I'm not giving you enough of it.

77. Different Strokes

My son, Matt, is a pretty good skateboarder. He's appeared in several Truth T-shirt video ads, doing his tricks (if you've seen any of them, he's the curly-haired guy skating down stair railings and doing back flips off the trunk of a tree). He's won trophies, appeared at skate demonstrations, and has even been featured on ESPN-2. As far as the skateboard goes, there's nothing he won't try. I've seen him skate up to a park bench, jump over it, and land on his skateboard on the other side. I'm pretty sure he did it on purpose. A park bench is hard to miss.

I used to skateboard when I was a teenager, too, but all I did was ride it. No fancy tricks or dangerous maneuvers. I just skated—boring, I know, but it got me where I needed to go.

Some of us live out our faith like that. We don't want to push ourselves to try anything beyond our comfort zone. We're afraid of falling on our face or making a fool of ourselves, so we just stand on the board and faithfully roll along, so to speak.

Others of us are more daring. We want to give life everything we've got. We're not afraid to take a few chances and see what happens. If we take a tumble, we're quick to get up and try it again and again, until we get it right.

Whichever way you choose to live your life, one way isn't any better than the next. I've never been on *X-treme Sports*, but I didn't get that many bruises either. My son, on the other hand, has taken some risks and pulled his share of tendons, but he has some nice trophies for his efforts. So, live a quiet, steadfast life of faith or be out in the forefront, daring and bold, whichever suits your personality best. Each of the twelve disciples had his own distinct ministry style. We are free to have our own style, too.

Thoughts to Ponder

When it comes to sharing your faith, would you say you're more daring or quiet?

Why do you think God needs all sorts of different personalities serving him?

Bumper Sticker for the Day

> **Only real people can share real faith.**

Scripture to Stand On

May all who seek you rejoice and be glad in you; may those who love your salvation always say, "The Lord be exalted!"

PSALM 40:16

Hello Again, Lord ...

Thank you, Lord, that I can be real with you.

78. What If ...?

What if everything we think doesn't matter to God, does?

What if he really doesn't like his name being used in vain, no matter how acceptable it has become in society?

What if he really does hate gossip as much as he hates murder?

What if he really does care about the homeless, regardless of our excuses for not caring?

What if we truly are going to be judged with the same measure of grace and forgiveness that we afford others?

What if it really is up to us to spread the gospel?

What if it really is all about grace and not about works?

What if he knows the true motive behind every good deed we have ever done?

What if we really do matter to God, even when we think we don't?

What if all the above is true?

It is.

Thoughts to Ponder

In what areas of your life have you been making excuses instead of taking God at his word?

Why do you think God wants us to take him at his word when it comes to both his grace and his commandments?

Bumper Sticker for the Day

> God is serious about his love ...
> and his law.

Scripture to Stand On

Blessed are all who fear the Lord, who walk in his ways.

PSALM 128:1

Hello Again, Lord ...

Lord, when it comes to your commandments, help me to remember we don't get to pick the best five out of ten.

79. In the Spotlight

Having directed numerous plays and comedy sketches for churches and schools, I've had the opportunity to work with many different spotlight operators. While they each had their own style and artistic eye, they all had one thing in common. Behind the light, they could barely be seen. Oh, you knew they were at their post because the light kept moving from one actor or scene to the next, but they themselves were well hidden in the shadows.

Some Christians are like spotlight operators. They shine the light on the cast around them, making sure to illuminate this one's missteps or that one's flawed character. As long as they can keep the spotlight shining on someone else, they figure they won't have to worry about their own act ever being exposed. Or so they think. Just as the houselights eventually come up in a play, sooner or later the houselights are going to come up in life and the spotlight operator won't be able to hide out in the shadows any longer. He'll have to face his own shortcomings and mistakes, and he'll be a more compassionate person because of it.

Thoughts to Ponder

Do you know someone who acts like a spiritual "spotlight operator"?

Why do you think it's important to regularly shine the light on our own lives?

Bumper Sticker for the Day

> **Find your own faults.**
> **Save your enemies the trouble.**

Scripture to Stand On

Would not God have discovered it, since he knows the secrets of the heart?

PSALM 44:21

Hello Again, Lord ...

Lord, remind me that if I spent the proper amount of time examining my own life, I'd have no time to examine the lives of those around me.

80. 'Fraid Not

For the last few months, Mark Lowry and I have been collecting answers to survey questions from his ReMarkables (the 30,000+ people on his mailing list). We've been asking different questions and getting their responses.

The very first question was, "If you could do anything at all, and knew you wouldn't fail, what would it be?" We were amazed by the number of people who had felt a call of God on their life to "work with the learning disabled," "become a missionary," "work with youth," "begin a prison ministry," "do something to help stop abuse of the elderly," and the like, all worthy causes. So, what was keeping them from doing what they had been called to do? Apparently, fear of failing.

If we allowed our fear of failure to determine how we lived our lives, none of us would get much accomplished. We'd never learn how to drive a car, because we might forget to signal a left turn someday. We'd never even attempt to work on a computer, because if we ever accidentally deleted a document, we'd never forgive ourselves. We'd have to stay in bed all day, because if we dressed ourselves and accidentally mismatched our socks, people would laugh at us. We'd never learn to cook, because we might incinerate the meal (or in my case, the kitchen). And forget ever talking on the telephone. What if we misdialed?

Do you realize that just about everything you've learned to do in life came with a degree of failure? That's how the learning process is. It's how we figure what not to do, then don't do it the next time. Very rarely does success come on our first attempt at anything.

It has been said that success isn't measured by how many

times we fall down, but by how many times we get up. If we're truly following God's will for our lives, we already have his guarantee that we'll eventually succeed.

Thoughts to Ponder

Is there something that you've been allowing a fear of failure to keep you from doing?

When it comes to God's call on our lives, why do you think it's important to overcome our fears and "just do it"?

Bumper Sticker for the Day

> Fear—the imaginary wall
> between ordinary and great.

Scripture to Stand On

Know that the Lord is God. It is he who made us, and we are his; we are his people, the sheep of his pasture.

PSALM 100:3

Hello Again, Lord ...

Lord, give me the courage to be everything you've planned for me to be.

81. Pastoral Buffet

In my new book of comedy sketches, there's one that takes place at a French restaurant. The customers seated at one table are poring over their menu. These folks are in a quandary: What should they have for Sunday dinner? Everything looks so tempting! How about Choir Director au Gratin, or a nice Evangelist Casserole?

Have you ever had your pastor (or others on the church staff) for dinner? I'm not talking about having them over for Sunday pot roast. They'd probably enjoy that. I'm talking about making them the "main course" of dinner conversation—you know, between mouthfuls of mashed potatoes and gravy. Whether you steam them or grill them, God doesn't like it. It may sound like fun, but God warns us in Psalms not to touch his anointed. He cautions us to not do his prophets any harm.

Many Christians overlook this passage. They figure it's open season on the pastor. If he does or says something they don't like, they feel justified in serving him for Sunday dinner. But ministers aren't called to be our table conversation. Believe it or not, they have a higher calling.

That's not to say they're perfect. There are plenty of stories in the news about men and women of the cloth who have fallen. When they're involved in behaviors that they clearly shouldn't be involved in, then they need to be held accountable to the church body. Most of the time, though, the criticism a pastor faces doesn't have anything to do with morality. It's usually over his personality, his family, or his preaching style. We criticize him because his sermons are too short, too long, too dry, too lively. We wish he'd be at the church more, be at home with his family more, visit the sick more, do more evangelism, start a building program, end a building program—whatever he does, we can usually find something to complain about.

God didn't intend for his ministers to have to go through such discouragement, especially from the people they have been sent to shepherd. So the next time we feel like taking a bite out of God's anointed, maybe we ought to look for something else on the menu. I'm sure the pastor will appreciate it. And so will God.

Thoughts to Ponder
Do you feel you are too critical of your pastor or youth minister?

Instead of criticizing people in the ministry, what should we be doing?

Bumper Sticker for the Day

> **Don't bite the hand that leads you.**

Scripture to Stand On
Do not touch my anointed ones; do my prophets no harm.

PSALM 105:15

Hello, Again, Lord ...
Lord, when I pray for my pastor may it be more than saying grace over him before I start chewing him up.

82. Hiding Out

I visited some caverns once that were supposed to have been where Jesse James and some of his gang used to hide out when they were running from the law. They'd ride their horses to some secret entrance, then slip inside the cavern unnoticed. Once inside, there were plenty of nooks and crannies in which they could hide. It was a little cool inside, but they'd be away from the elements, and there were plenty of pools of water. It seemed like the perfect place to hide out.

When Jonah was running from God, he thought he'd found the perfect place to hide out, too—on a boat headed for Tarshish. God sent a storm along, though, and soon the others in the boat concluded that Jonah must be their problem and cast him overboard. God then provided a big fish to come along and swallow him whole. Not your regular bed-and-breakfast, but God is a creative God.

From inside the belly of that fish, Jonah must have done a lot of thinking, just as the James gang must have done a lot of thinking. They must have wondered if all the running was worth it.

After three days, Jonah decided he'd had enough. He didn't like sushi all that much anyway, and running from God was getting him nowhere. He repented and God caused the big fish to spit him out onto dry ground. Jonah went on to Ninevah, successfully completing the mission to which he was called.

Jesse James, on the other hand, continued to live the life he had been living. Whatever thinking he might have been doing down in those caverns didn't do anything to change him. He maintained his life of lawlessness and eventually died of a gunshot wound in the back.

There may be times in your life when you feel like running away. There may be times when God even allows you to get to a place where he can have your undivided attention. When he does, listen. It could be your ticket out of hiding. It might even be a last opportunity to turn your life around.

Thoughts to Ponder

Have you ever tried hiding from God?

How do you think God feels when we try to hide from him?

Bumper Sticker for the Day

> Running *from* God doesn't solve a thing.
> But running *to* him does.

Scripture to Stand On

Where can I go from your Spirit? Where can I flee from your presence?

PSALM 139:7

Hello, Again, Lord ...

Lord, may I always give you my undivided attention before you have to take it.

83. Failed Again

Is there someone in your life for whom it seems you can do nothing right? No matter how hard you try to be perfect, this person figures it's his or her calling in life to find something for which to criticize you. It's almost as if this person is hoping you'll fail so he or she can say, "See, I knew you couldn't do it!"

Dealing with someone like that, especially on a daily basis, can be frustrating. It can drive you either to fulfill the expectations and fail, or to achieve beyond your wildest dreams, but still feel empty inside. It's a lose-lose proposition.

Failing isn't something you want to do, but because of someone's constant criticism and negative predictions, you might feel you have to just to please that person. If you're accomplishing things only so someone will take notice, and he or she still doesn't, you'll forever feel cheated, frustrated, and unhappy with yourself.

The answer, therefore, isn't in failing or in more and more accomplishments. The answer is for *you* to be happy with yourself. If *you're* proud of *you*, it won't matter who else is proud of you. You'll know your own worth, in spite of what others may say or do.

So be proud of yourself. Know what you're capable of accomplishing and what you've already accomplished. If no one else sees it, you don't have to rent a billboard to announce it. You'll know it down deep inside of you, and that's where it counts, anyway.

Thoughts to Ponder

Whom do you allow to determine your worth?

Is there someone in your life who seems to want you to fail? What do you think this person's motive might be?

Bumper Sticker for the Day

> **Need a pat on the back?**
> **Use your own hand if necessary.**

Scripture to Stand On

The Lord sustains the humble but casts the wicked to the ground.

PSALM 147:6

Hello, Again, Lord ...

Lord, thank you that those who would want me to fail have to get through you first.

84. Open Arms

Is being a Christian about following rules, or having the heart of Christ? Actually, it's both. Granted, we're supposed to follow God's rules. They're for our own good. But following rules without having the heart of Christ is the problem Jesus saw in the Pharisees. They were rule followers, yet failed miserably in the areas of compassion, mercy, and grace.

Jesus wanted his followers to have his heart. He told us that in so many of his parables. Take the one about the Prodigal Son. When the boy finally came home, his father didn't give him a lecture, saying, "See, I knew you were going to squander all of your money! You have to learn everything the hard way, don't you? Why do I even bother trying to help you?" No. The father received the boy with open arms. He knew his son had sinned against him, and he was by no means condoning that rebellion. But he didn't rub his son's nose in it, listing his wrongs one by one. He simply forgave him.

When the woman who was caught in adultery was going to be stoned, Jesus didn't say, "Sorry, dear, but there's nothing I can do. You chose this lifestyle, and now you have to pay the price for your loose behavior." Instead, he confronted her accusers, reminding them that they had their own sins to answer for. Then he forgave the woman and told her to "Go and sin no more."

Jesus was the only one who had a right to condemn the woman because of his sinlessness, yet he was the only one who offered her mercy. In front of all those people, he could have easily made her an example of the price for sin. Instead, he made her an example of his love.

Thoughts to Ponder

Have you ever been guilty of throwing a stone at someone else?

Why do you think Jesus felt it was important to point out that none of us are worthy enough to judge another?

Bumper Sticker for the Day

Instead of throwing stones,
next time try throwing a little mercy around.

Scripture to Stand On

The Lord is compassionate and gracious, slow to anger, abounding in love.

PSALM 103:8

Hello, Again, Lord ...

Lord, before I throw a stone at someone else, help me to see the boulder that could be aimed at me.

85. Gimme, Gimme, Gimme

Do you have a "To Do" list for God? Do you write down all the things you want him to do for you? Does it look something like this:

1. Lord, I know I don't have a job, but I really need a car—you know, 'cause all my friends have one. So, send me a car, God. Any car. OK, well, not just any car. That new red Mustang I saw on the car lot today. You said you'd supply all my needs, Lord, and I really neeeeeeed that car. See what you can do, OK? Amen. P.S. I forgot to mention, I'd like the white interior, too. Nothing's impossible for you, Lord. Right?

2. I could really use your help getting me through my finals, too, Lord. I didn't have time to study. My friends kept calling me ... OK, I kept calling them ... and I had to do my nails, and all my soaps kept having those cliffhanger endings. I had to tune in every day to see what was going to happen next. I'm not omniscient like you. Well, anyway, I need you to give me instant recall for all the right answers. No, you'd better make that divine revelation. Since I didn't input any information, it wouldn't really be considered "recall," would it? So can you help me out, Lord?

3. Another thing I'd really like is front-row tickets to that big concert this Friday night. Can I have 'em, huh, God, can I? I'll never ask for another thing ... uh, I mean, other than what's on these daily lists. But I really do want to go to that concert!

Our "To Do" list can go on for pages, but you get the picture. If we're not careful, we can treat the Creator of the universe like our errand boy. Maybe it's time we were a little more concerned with *his* "To Do" list for us, and a little less concerned with our own desires. God has promised to meet our needs, but there are a lot of things we beg for that we really can do without.

Thoughts to Ponder

When you think about your prayer life lately, would you say you've been doing more asking than listening?

Why do you think God wants us to ask what he has on his "To Do" list for us?

Bumper Sticker for the Day

> **"Thy will be done" and "My will be done" aren't the same prayer.**

Scripture to Stand On

Turn my eyes away from worthless things; renew my life according to your word.

PSALM 119:37

Hello, Again, Lord ...

Lord, help me to remember that your power to do anything isn't a promise to do everything I want. Sometimes what I want isn't what's best for me.

86. A Faithful Friend

It's easy to criticize the disciples for not standing up for Jesus when he was being falsely accused before Pilate. But how often do we abandon our own friends in their time of need? When's the last time you were involved in a conversation where you heard someone say, "Hey, that's my friend and I won't let you talk about her that way"?

Usually, we just take it all in. It may be rumors, false accusations, or biased opinions, but instead of defending, we listen. Instead of being loyal friends, we're wishy-washy ones.

Just as in the time of Christ, people tend to think of themselves first. They don't want to risk anything by standing up for a friend. The disciples would have risked certain death had they stood up for their friend Jesus. They probably wanted to be loyal, but they didn't have the courage. The bottom line is, Jesus had no one to come to his defense. It was, of course, all part of God's plan, but it still must have hurt Jesus. These were eleven men whom he had considered friends. He had even considered Judas a friend, and Judas sold him out for just thirty pieces of silver.

How much are your friends worth to you? How much is Jesus worth? How much courage do you have to stand up for those you love?

Thoughts to Ponder

Do you feel you're a loyal friend?

If you had been alive at the time of Jesus' trial, do you think you would have been able to stand up for him in the midst of that angry mob?

Bumper Sticker for the Day

> **A friendship easily surrendered probably never existed in the first place.**

Scripture to Stand On

Thus they have rewarded me evil for good, and hatred for my love.

PSALM 109:5, NKJV

Hello, Again, Lord ...

Lord, when a friend is being persecuted, help me to stand by him, and not just stand by.

87. Divine Encounters

With the popularity of the television series "Touched by an Angel," more and more stories of real encounters with angels are coming forth. I can't say for certain whether I've ever had one myself, but I do know that my family and I have had numerous encounters with people who were on a heavenly mission—people who came along with an encouraging word at the precise moment we needed it or who provided for a financial need just in the nick of time. These were needs that no one else could have possibly known about, so there's no doubt in our minds that God had ordered the steps of the messengers.

What is most amazing about these encounters is the people God chose to use. They weren't the people I would have expected our help or encouragement to come from. Had God used a close friend, or relative, we could have easily dismissed it as a human act of kindness. But because our help came from people I hardly knew, there was no way it was anything other than a divine intervention in our time of need.

Frankly, I think God enjoys seeing the looks on our faces when our help comes from an unexpected source. While we're waiting for help to come from one place, he's busy arranging for it to come from another. Maybe that's so we'll never doubt who the real source of our help is.

Thoughts to Ponder

Have you ever received help or encouragement from someone whom you knew was sent by God?

Has God ever led you to do something specific for someone in need?

Bumper Sticker for the Day

> **You don't have to be an angel
> to do angelic things.**

Scripture to Stand On

I lift up my eyes to the hills—where does my help come from?

PSALM 121:1

Hello, Again, Lord ...

Lord, thank you that your help is always just what's needed and always on time.

88. Time Flies

When we're busy, it's amazing how quickly time passes. We get on the Internet after dinner and before we know it, it's almost midnight. Or we stop off at the mall at 6:00, and after what to us seems like an hour we're hearing them announce over the P.A. that it's 9:00 and the store is closing. Where did the time go? The same place it's always gone. Away.

Time doesn't speed up because we're busy or slow down when we're bored. It passes at the same rate at which it always passes—sixty seconds a minute, sixty minutes an hour, twenty-four hours a day.

If we're not careful, though, we can get so busy with school, work, friends, or whatever, that we don't see how quickly our lives are passing. One day we're teenagers and just a few years later (it seems) we're thirty, forty, or even fifty years old. We'll look back on our lives and wonder where all those years went.

That's why we need to savor each moment as it comes. We only have so much time here on earth, and none of us knows exactly how much. We need to pay attention and be a part of our own lives. We don't want to be so busy that we don't see the time passing, that we don't make every moment count, that we don't accomplish what it is we're meant to accomplish. We don't want the clock striking midnight when we think we've still got plenty of time left in the day.

Thoughts to Ponder

Do you feel you're living life to the fullest?

In what ways do you think you could make better use of the time you've been given?

Bumper Sticker for the Day

> Life is like a stew—
> the more you put in, the better it is.

Scripture to Stand On

He asked you for life, and you gave it to him—length of days, for ever and ever.

PSALM 21:4

Hello, Again, Lord ...

Lord, may I show my appreciation for your gift of life by making every moment count.

89. Take a Hike

I'm not much of a hiker. Whenever I get conned into taking a hike, I try to make sure someone else is in the lead, preferably someone who has walked the trail before, an experienced guide. The reason for this is simple—self-preservation. I don't want to get lost out in the wilderness and have to wait for someone to finally notice the buzzards circling overhead to locate me. I want to be sure that wherever I hike to, the Domino's pizza delivery boy will be able to find me. I don't want to unknowingly walk into a quicksand pit, or become the moving target for an archery team practicing for the Olympics.

Being an inexperienced hiker, there's no way for me to know all the things that I need to watch out for. With a guide leading me, however, someone who's walked the trail hundreds of times, I won't have to worry about any of these things.

God is our experienced guide on our hike through life. He knows where the quicksand pits are and can easily steer us clear of them if we'll only listen. He knows where the enemy's arrows are going to be flying and can protect us from those, too. If we stay close at his side, he'll make sure we stay on the trail, and we'll never have to worry whether we're headed in the right direction.

Thoughts to Ponder

Why do you think we sometimes try to second-guess our "guide"?

Have you ever been totally lost? How did it make you feel?

Bumper Sticker for the Day

> **The best time to ask directions
> is before we get lost.**

Scripture to Stand On

I will praise the Lord, who counsels me; even at night my heart instructs me.

PSALM 16:7

Hello, Again, Lord ...

Lord, help me to remember that you not only know the trail, you formed the mountain.

90. The Real You

Who are you when no one's looking? When there's no audience to impress or disappoint? When you're alone in your room, away from your friends and family? Who are you when there aren't any outside influences, when you're free to be yourself, to question your own motives, to analyze your own shortcomings and strong points?

Who are you? Answer the following questions as though you were doing it totally anonymously, and you are, because the answers will be only in your head.

What motivates your good behavior? (a) fear of punishment; (b) desire to do good; (c) a need to impress others; (d) other.

What motivates your bad behavior? (a) peer pressure; (b) rebellion; (c) a need for attention; (d) other.

What one thing do you like best about your personality? What one thing do you like least?

Why do you hang out with the friends you do? (a) they're encouraging and bring out the best in me; (b) I'm afraid of having no friends; (c) I know they're not good for me, but I don't know how to break the ties; (d) other.

Even if you fail at it, what would you like to be when you grow up?

What usually keeps you from pursuing the goals you have for yourself?

What one thing do you wish you could forget?

What are you most afraid of?

If you had the world's attention for five minutes, and you were still anonymous, what would you say?

The above questions are just a springboard to others that you might ask yourself. You've met and will continue to meet a lot of people throughout your lifetime. Maybe it's time you got to know one of them a little more intimately.

Thoughts to Ponder
Do you feel you're free to be who you really are?

If not, what's keeping you from being yourself?

Bumper Sticker for the Day

> **Some people are best friends
> with everyone but themselves.**

Scripture to Stand On
Search me, O God, and know my heart; test me and know my anxious thoughts.

PSALM 139:23

Hello, Again, Lord ...
Lord, help me to become the person you've planned for me to be.

God walks
inside you thru
every situation in
life that you face—
He is your strength and
joy.

In Jesus' love,
Jordi :)